BARRON'S ART HANDBOOKS

ILLUSTRATION
TECHNIQUES

BARRON'S

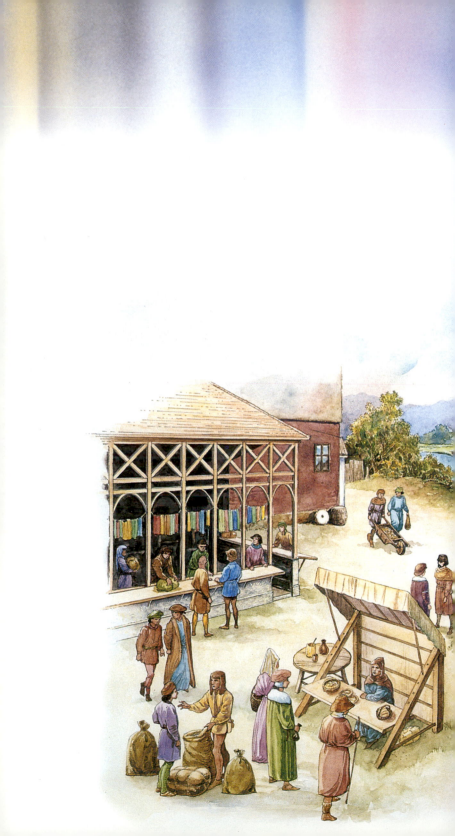

BARRON'S ART HANDBOOKS

ILLUSTRATION
TECHNIQUES

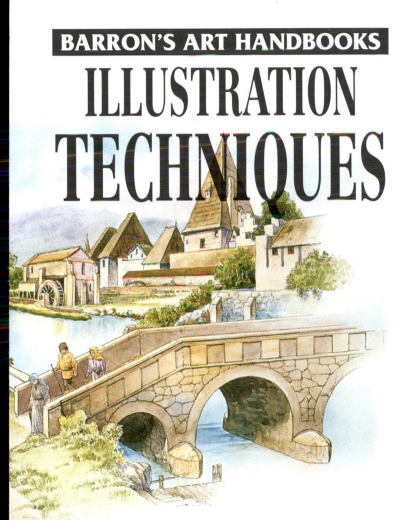

BARRON'S

CONTENTS

ILLUSTRATION THROUGHOUT HISTORY

The antecedents of illustration as we know it today were the miniatures that medieval artists used to decorate manuscripts. These miniatures were replaced by engravings at the start of the Renaissance. Modern illustrating began with the invention of the printing press and the ability to print series of images.

Medieval Manuscripts

Medieval manuscripts contain the earliest examples of illustrations. These illustrations involve filigree and hand-painted images that complement the texts by ornamenting them in extremely inventive ways. Among the most impressive works are the capital letters of the Irish gospels. (Among them are the celebrated Lindisfarne Gospel from the tenth century, one of the most ancient in all of Europe.) The miniatures were very detailed and minute, created with great care. They frequently attained the status of true works of art.

The Development of Engraving

Ever since the Renaissance, styles of illustrating have developed hand in hand with technical advances in the reproduction of images. Starting with the invention of the printing press, engravings were always on wood. They incorporated image and text on the same plate. Up to the nineteenth century, when new methods of engraving on wood revived this specialty, the technique of engraving on wood did not facilitate including fine detail. Precision became possible with the start of engraving on metal plates, which started in the sixteenth century. It required printing the image and the text separately, which brought full-page, freestanding illustrations and large-format works into popularity. This technique initiated a magnificent era in engraved plates (realistic portraits, geographic maps, scientific illustrations, on so on). That use of engraving has survived to this day (dry point, etching, aquatint, and others), although it is now limited to the work of actual artists rather than illustrators. The next great innovation was illustration in lithographic stone (invented in 1798). Unlike previous engravings that had to be colored by hand, it led to color printing, an antecedent of the modern photogravure techniques currently in use.

Martyrology of Gesualdo *(ca. 1400). Museu Diocesà de Girona (Spain).*
The art of calligraphy was joined to the illustrator's art in the medieval codices.

William Hogarth, The Lesson. *National Chalcography, Madrid (Spain). Hogarth was the most important of the satirical illustrators of the eighteenth century.*

The Splendor of the Eighteenth Century

The tremendous impetus that book illustration received in the eighteenth century, thanks to the cultural diffusion of the illustrated intellectual publications in France and England, also extended to magazines and other periodicals, which are much more common nowadays. In England, the genre of political and social satire appeared, which developed into one of the most popular forms of illustration in the modern world. The best English satirist was William Hogarth (1697–1764). His wonderful engravings caricature the vices and miseries of English urban society of the eighteenth century and its political system. In France, his counterpart a century later was Honoré Daumier (1808–1879), who became embroiled in serious legal problems for satirizing Louis Philippe d'Orléans in a series of famous caricatures. Both artists were great painters. However, during their lifetimes, they were known mainly for their work as illustrators.

Honoré Daumier, Gargantua. *Daumier was one of the best painters of his era, but he became famous for his appealing illustrations, generally satirical in nature. This is one of the caricatures of Louis Philippe d'Orléans that got him into difficulties with the law in France.*

MODERN AND CONTEMPORARY ILLUSTRATION

The great revolution in modern illustration came with the introduction of color reproduction in the second half of the nineteenth century. First silk screen printing and then three- and four-color printing made possible the standardization of a process that previously had to be carried out by hand. Since that time, the diffusion of illustrations has become a ubiquitous phenomenon.

Poster Art

The second half of the nineteenth century was the pinnacle of poster art and all types of graphic propaganda. Many authors consider that poster art was born in France around the middle of the nineteenth century at the hands of two great painters: Honoré Daumier (1808–1879) and Édouard Manet (1832–1883). The style of these two artists and their followers marked the aesthetics of what would become decorative modernism. The evolution of illustrating at the end of the nineteenth century reached its apogee in the works of Toulouse-Lautrec (1864–1901). Bonnard (1867–1947) and Steinlen (1859–1923) were some of the other noted artists whose posters and illustrations for magazines and literary works were

Théophile Alexandre Steinlen. The Conversion of Angela (illustration for the Gil-Blas Seminary). Steinlen was the most famous and influential illustrator of his generation.

milestones effectively defining the social and cultural aesthetic of the time.

Narrative Illustrations

In the nineteenth century, illustrators were immersed in the realistic and humorous tradition established by the great Victorian artists. The nucleus of that tradition was rigorous academic drawing, even when the illustration was intended to be decorative or comical or when done for works intended for

Aubrey Beardsley. This wonderful illustration characterizes the subject perfectly without showing his facial features.

Arthur Rackham. His silhouettes, despite their apparent simplicity, conceal a refined ornamental playfulness that makes them very attractive and explicit from the narrative point of view.

children. One of the best examples of this tendency, which remained in force during the first decades of the twentieth century (and which continues to this day), is the delightful silhouettes of the English illustrator Arthur Rackham (1867–1939). The Frenchman Gustave Doré (1832–1883) and the Englishman Aubrey Beardsley (1872–1898) were the most famous illustrators of their respective countries as a result of their masterful recreations of literary episodes—engravings in the case of Doré and pen-and-ink illustrations with Beardsley.

From the Start of the Twentieth Century to the Present Time

In the 1920s and 1930s, a new application came into favor among editors and publicists; it was an outgrowth of the new idioms used by avant-garde painters and sculptors. The postwar economic expansion gave the most restless illustrators an opportunity to work in more modern and expressive ways. It was a type of illustrating calculated to capture the spirit of the new age: the age of mass communication, of new media, and of consumer society.

The new illustration went beyond the obligatory supremacy of faithful and figurative drawing. It opened up an exploration of purely visual effects that approached abstract art. It also paved the way for photomontage and new techniques made possible by modern equipment, such as airbrush painting, which opened up the field of large-format illustrations.

Impressionism and Symbolism

Two crucial artistic movements coexisted in the last decades of the nineteenth century: impressionism and symbolism. The former was a foil to realism, with themes drawn from everyday life and with a quick and sketchy style. Symbolism, on the other hand, worked with literary and fantastic themes in an extremely refined and decorative style. Both schools boasted many first-rate illustrators whose influence continues even today.

Alexandre de Riquer. Modernist poster that summarizes the graphic aesthetic of art nouveau at the end of the nineteenth century.

CONCEPTUAL ILLUSTRATION

This label is applied to all types of illustration that are not dictated by data from some text, a literary theme, or other information but that develop a personal concept born of the illustrator's ideas surrounding the theme to be illustrated. Conceptual illustrations are the ones that afford the broadest range for the professional's creativity and personal style.

Creative Illustrations

Conceptual illustration is essentially creative. A large measure of its success is rooted in the style of the illustrator.

Conceptual illustration represents general ideas rather than individual facts; the illustrator has to know the editorial line of the publication to make his or her work fit in. A conceptual image must be graphically bold and captured quickly, but it should not influence the reader's experience by offering an excessively personal point of view. Whatever the illustrator's style, it must have fine visual quality and be somewhat different and much more specific than the general pictorial or artistic quality. Conceptual illustration creates a climate for reading or gives the readers expectations about what they may find in the text as well as offering a general glimpse of the contents.

Technical Resources

Most cultural or general interest magazines rely on a regular series of illustrators who create the periodical's public image. Many of these illustrators even do the cover art. The style of many of these professionals can be characterized more by personal and inventive use of technique than by skill in representation. Conceptual illustrations admit nearly abstract styles in which the ornamental qualities of the material used (very frequently pastel but also India ink and collage) become the center of interest. By working with these mediums, conceptual illustrators can characterize a theme by means of slight changes in the distribution of forms and colors.

MORE ON THIS SUBJECT

• Illustrating as a Profession p. 26

Conceptual creations are true creations that complete and impart a personal graphic version of the text that they illustrate.

This work by Ramón de Jesús, with its pronounced dreamy atmosphere, is an excellent example of technical invention in the service of a conceptual illustration.

This decorative illustration done by Myriam Ferrón was created to accompany a book about the history of ancient Egypt.

Decorative Illustrations

Decorative illustration is used to embellish pages of text. It usually consists of marginal illustrations that enrich the graphic design of the publication (flyleaves, abstract forms or spots, objects and details that are mentioned in the text, and so on). Ornamental illustration is the oldest form of illustration (capital letters, manuscripts, and others). It is intimately connected to the general development of book and magazine printing. It usually functions as a technical, didactic, or documentary complement. Decorative illustration can also reinforce explanations in the text, including details that have a particular visual appeal.

Cover Illustrations

Cover art requires the maximum graphic power on the part of the illustrators, whether they are granted total liberty or must conform to parameters clearly set by an editor. Cover art must be done in harmony with the overall design of the book. It sometimes covers the entire dust jacket and sets the tone for the illustrations in the whole work. Cover illustrations can also involve labeling of texts or their typography. In many cases, the complexity of the illustration is a function of the size of the individual cover, which may be for a conventional book or a compact disc.

John Heartfield. Novel cover (detail). Collection IVAM-Marco Pinkus, Valencia (Spain). Heartfield was a master of photomontage. His graphic talent is embodied in this conceptual image.

ADVERTISING ART

Advertising art is designed to complement or give form and personality to a product or commercial brand or to announce an event. Often the works can be adapted to different formats, according to the medium that the publicist uses (posters, book covers, containers, magazine pages, and so on). The main characteristic of advertising art is its immediate and forceful visual impact.

Commercial Images

Advertising images are usually widely distributed and are highly visible. The public perception of a product depends on them to a great degree. The commercial importance of these works requires the company that commissions the illustrator's services to specify some very precise parameters. The artistic director studies and evaluates the original works very carefully, and they are subjected to the scrutiny of various officials in the company. This set of factors leads many companies to contract with advertising agencies or graphic design departments,

Commercial illustration by Miquel Ferrón designed to complement the public image and packaging for a line of food products.

Airbrush illustration by Miquel Ferrón. Commercial images need to have a special visual power to compete with the accumulation of images that inundate urban societies.

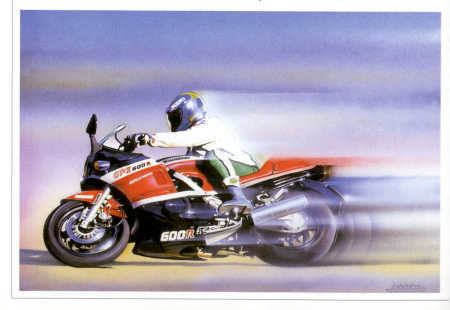

Poster Art

Producing posters has a lot in common with producing book covers (sometimes book covers are edited like advertising). However, posters require even more graphic brilliance because they have to compete with many other visual ads. Nowadays, few posters are based on conventional illustration because photography and computer illustration techniques have taken over that arena, which was once reserved for painters and illustrators.

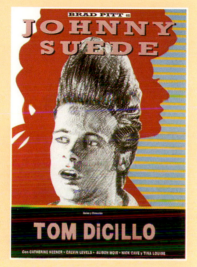

Santi Erill, poster for a movie. *Movie poster done in collage, filled with graphic interest and done using very simple means.*

Fashion Illustrating

Fashion illustrating has not been supplanted by photography. Its usefulness ranges from inspiration for the illustrator to the expression of a characteristic style applicable to fashion books, magazines, and general advertising. Fashion illustrating is highly stylized. It is usually entrusted to specialists who can highlight the qualities of color and texture of fabric and the way it flows and folds and who can do this elegantly and spectacularly. The techniques used for fashion illustrating tend to be rapid and practically require virtuosity in using the materials.

which, in turn, contact the illustrator. In exceptional cases, the job is consigned to a well-known artist. Then the hope is that the artist will capture a personal vision of the product rather than conform to precise criteria or specifications. In other instances, it is a simple question of format that distinguishes ad illustrations from other genres. For example, the majority of modern publishing houses enlarge and adapt the cover designs for their books so they can be used as advertising posters.

Packaging

Illustrations for *packaging* (wrappings and presentations of commercial products) convey an image of a worldwide brand and are applied with minor variations to different types of containers, wrappers, and accessories that a brand exposes to the public (labels, food product lines, public places, and others). There is no definite line in this type of project. Each business usually commissions illustrations that harmonize with its logo or, in case that image does not yet exist, works with graphic designers and illustrators to create one.

MORE ON THIS SUBJECT

• Conceptual Illustration p. 10

Fashion illustrations have an ornamental as well as an informational purpose and are an aesthetic advertisement for a commercial brand. Illustration by Josep Torres.

NARRATIVE ILLUSTRATIONS

Among the most common types of illustration are a few noteworthy ones whose task is to accomplish the graphic expression of a story line. Nowadays, providing illustrations for novels and tales is not as common as it used to be, but some genres and illustrations still depict an event or a sequence of events according to a written script or cinematographic type (graphic humor, comics, animation, and others).

Illustrations for Literary Works

A long tradition exists of tales in which the illustrations have become so popular that imagining these stories without the pictures that go along with them is difficult. Classical tales are always a temptation to editors because of their illustrative possibilities, but the job is risky. The reader naturally has a tendency to form a mental image of the characters, and faithfulness to detail can never be overlooked. Reconstructing a historic period is also necessary, and that requires lots of hard work in research and reconstruction. Usually, editors prefer not to get involved in this type of project and prefer to illustrate contemporary works.

Illustration for children by Anna Llorens. This is clearly a narrative illustration done in a style that is easy to interpret.

Graphic Humor

Graphic humor may be the most specialized type of illustration of all because it communicates the genius and the humor of a single individual by means of personalized graphics, generally in the

form of caricatures. This is a type of illustration in which the technical features are subordinated to cleverness and personal talent. Good graphic humorists are complete personalities in the field of periodicals. Their work enjoys greater loyalty among readers than does the work of the other magazine and literary collaborators. It also imparts a real trademark style to the publication.

Drawing by Ramón de Jesús. Graphic humor depends in large measure on the distinctive style of the illustrator; it has to be simple and transmit the gag with immediacy.

*Illustration by Charles Robinson for a fantasy story.
The characterization and setting of the work must be interpreted
by the narrative illustrator.*

activity book, and so on). Illustrations for children must be appealing to the youngsters. However, the children are not the direct consumers of these illustrations, but, rather, their parents are. Nor do the children commission the illustrations. The editors do so. This type of illustration has to satisfy the needs of the children without showing condescension; it has to take into account the requirements of the publication's plot and come up with the graphic resources that will call attention to them. At the same time, it has to be appealing to adults, for they are the ones who buy the books and read them. Illustrators for children's books must remember all this. Those who hold the key to this discipline are usually specialists whose style can be appreciated on different levels.

MORE ON THIS SUBJECT

• Modern and Contemporary Illustration p. 8

Illustrations for Children

Many types of books are available for children, ranging from the most elementary plots aimed at very young children to complex stories on a par with some literature for adults. Illustrations for textbooks for children also require as much documentation as the most demanding technical illustrations.

Illustration for young children is an immense field in which the age of the target audience is an important consideration. In general, illustrations for children's books have to provide a clear and understandable interpretation of the theme or plot, always in conjunction with the type of work involved (narrative, textbook,

Illustration by M. Àngels Comella. Illustrations for young children have to be more ideographic than narrative; in other words, they have to convey with total simplicity the fundamental elements or characters of the story being told.

COMICS

Comics are practically a world apart within illustration. The illustrator has to be able to interpret a script, convey it in a fairly cinematographic way, and create well-developed characters. A comics artist is not illustrating a book but, rather, is creating the entire work. Comics are a genre practiced by highly specialized illustrators who have a very special narrative talent as well as artistic ability.

Creating a comic strip requires good planning for every page. The illustrator has to take into account the rhythm of the story, the emphasis on situations and characters, and the graphic distribution of text and images. Page by Josep Torres.

Text and Images

Even though the majority of comic book illustrators work with scripts from someone else or adaptations of literary works, illustrators who specialize in this genre have to be capable of conveying the logical flow of a story's episodes in such a way that the drawings are as important as the story and are a true vehicle for the action. The creative process for comics is complex and involves many technical considerations that can be acquired only through practice. With but few exceptions, comics illustrators do not work on specific commission. Rather, they search out interesting plots themselves or collaborate with scriptwriters who adapt to their style to complete the works. Of course, the presence of the editor is very important. That person, in the final analysis, determines the direction of the publication in which the graphic stories will be published. Just the same, the editor always leaves up to the authors the type of story and the graphic style, as long as where the story is headed and how it will be adapted to the publication's requirements are clear.

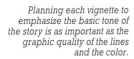

Planning each vignette to emphasize the basic tone of the story is as important as the graphic quality of the lines and the color.

Graphic Humor in Black and White

Practically all magazines that deal in general information include illustrations of graphic humor in their pages. The majority of newspapers and many magazines work with a single color (black). Illustrators who do this type of work have to keep clearly in mind the limitations of the medium, since too much detail almost always results in poor graphic quality. The artists have to be familiar with the text and discover the point where their style can produce an interesting illustration in harmony with the content.

most entirely on quick and flowing lines, and the shapes have to be produced with just a few strokes.

Many graphic humorists are capable of creating a situation with simple visual effects. These works are deceptively simple. In fact, they require a masterful application of line, form, and movement of the human figures, who always have to be immediately recog-

Comics, Graphic Humor, and Animation

Illustrations for comics and graphic humor usually require a special skill in constructing the drawing. Typically, illustrators who specialize in these genres work with nibs and artist's brushes to produce a drawing with direct appeal filled with spontaneity and freshness that the reader can understand quickly and that explains a situation very economically. The technique for these works is based al-

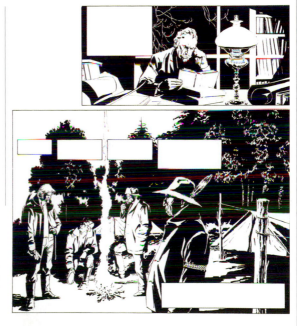

In comics, color is frequently applied in large blocks of flat color that maintain a visual balance on the entire page, as in this illustration by Josep Torres.

Some comics, such as this frame by Vicenç Ballestar, permit a freer and more pictorial visual quality that is much more akin to a quick sketch than to a diagram.

nizable to the reader, plus a long apprenticeship in drawing characters.

Still more specialized than comics and graphic humor is animation, which is usually done in teams. It is highly technical and involves minute preparation. Specialists do different parts of the same production. These jobs take lots of time, and they are the province of agencies or small companies rather than individual artists. Nowadays, animation always involves using a computer.

SCIENTIFIC ILLUSTRATION

Scientific illustration is one of the most effective mediums for presenting precise and detailed information about subjects that require significant visual support. Despite the modern technology available to artists, scientific illustration is one of the areas where advances in photographic reproduction have done nothing to displace the work of graphic artists.

Evolution of Scientific Illustration

Illustrations intended for reproduction have traditionally been engraved on wood (figurative images) or on copper plates (cartography and very precise documentary images). Frequently, these printed images were colored with watercolors after printing.

In the eighteenth century, scientific illustration made spectacular advances thanks to the initiative of the encyclopedists, who needed lots of graphic material to illustrate their huge reference works. The advances in techniques of reproduction, and especially the appearance of photomechanical reproduction at the end of the nineteenth century, allowed a tremendously broad distribution of all kinds of illus-

Illustration from the book The Formation of Rainbows *(1771) by J. J. Scheuchzer. The first modern scientific illustrations were engraved and colored by hand.*

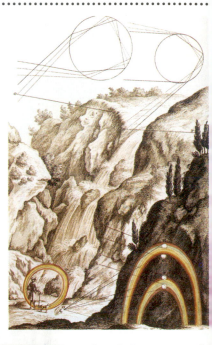

trations. At that moment, technical illustration reached one of its apogees with what was known as *presentation illustrations* of mechanical devices and architectural structures. These works were carefully colored by hand on very detailed engravings. Their purpose was to offer a precise and attractive view of the project under consideration rather than to serve as a reference for the builder. The introduc-

Illustrations intended for works of broad distribution must exhibit a visual brilliance that is not necessary in specialized publications. Work by Antonio Muñoz.

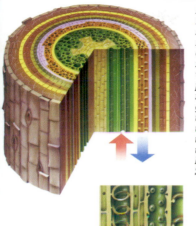

Frequently, scientific illustrations have to specify certain features and details clearly that, in reality, are scarcely visible. For that purpose, the requirements are good planning of the chosen view, the drawing, and the colors to be used. Illustration: Marcel Socias Studio.

tion in the twentieth century of airbrush technique and computer-assisted illustration, combined with the development of photomechanical reproduction techniques, made possible a superior brilliancy of color and maximum precision in reproducing the artists' original works.

Scientific Images

Scientific images require on the part of the illustrator a different interpretation of the information to be conveyed, both with respect to the important data of the subject and the style used to represent them. Illustrating a magazine for mass distribution and general interest is something quite different than illustrating a specialized journal. In the latter case, the readers do not expect spectacular images but, rather, visual clarifications of the concepts put forth in the text. General interest publications, like textbooks for students, require greater visual brilliance and offer the illustrator more creative freedom.

Representations of the Invisible

Very frequently, the illustrator has to provide a clear visual representation of something invisible to photography (viruses, atoms, magnetism, physiological processes, and others). In this type of illustration, the graphic documentation can proceed only from other illustrations, unless the illustrator feels capable of correctly interpreting all the scientific data to produce a credible and scientifically plausible image.

In the majority of the cases, contrasting the image with anything more coherent is impossible. So, the artist has quite a lot of creative latitude.

MORE ON THIS SUBJECT

- Illustration Throughout History p. 6
- Modern and Contemporary Illustration p. 8

Graphic Synthesis

The majority of medical, anatomical, botanical, and geological illustrations are a synthesis based on a large amount of information. This synthesis needs to be visually clear and to avoid both redundancy and extraneous details. A balance between realism and legibility is the key to success for these works. A high degree of realism may interfere with distinguishing the important details from the unimportant ones, whereas excessively schematic illustrations may trivialize the reality of the objects depicted.

Medical works are one type of publication that cannot do without specialized illustrators. Drawing by Miquel Ferrón.

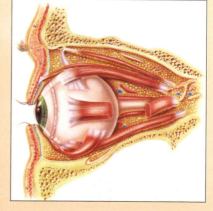

TECHNICAL ILLUSTRATION

Advances in technology and the sciences in general call for clear representations that are truly useful as dependable references about the mechanism, the components, and the specific functions of a machine, an organism, or a natural system. In reality, computers are a tremendous aid to artists. However, traditional mediums are still used that require more expertise on the part of the illustrator than computer power.

Characteristics

The essential characteristic of technical illustrations is clarity and legibility of the information that they communicate. No matter how complex and detailed one of these illustrations may be, the reader has to be able to identify the important elements. All details need to be in their precise location in the whole and be presented in the correct shape and proportion. Still more is needed. This type of illustration has to be visually appealing and interesting. Its graphic quality (form, color, and contrast) also has to be on a par with the information it conveys.

Mechanical Drawings

Mechanical drawings are highly specialized illustrations that usually adhere to far more concrete guidelines than any other type of illustration. Almost all of them require representations on a fixed scale and specific views of the elements pictured. Within this division are also included cross-sectional and exploded

Mastery of Techniques

Technical illustrations require that the artist possess total mastery of realistic drawing as well as of different systems representating scale and perspective. To these basic skills one must add a rigorous and methodical attitude in performing the work and a certain graphic talent for producing the best and most attractive representation of the subject. Most technical illustrators began their careers working in professional studios, where they picked up the experience and the skills essential to begin their careers as independent illustrators.

Jean Dubreuil, engraving from the book Practical Perspective. *Architectural perspectives require that the artist have a solid familiarity with representational systems.*

MORE ON THIS SUBJECT

- Illustration Throughout History p. 6
- Modern and Contemporary Illustration p. 8
- Scientific Illustration p. 18

drawings—illustrations of some mechanical device that show all the device's parts located in the proper place but at varying levels or distances. Other possibilities include relief views or illustrations done as overhead views in perspective (architectural structures, interiors, vehicles, mechanical parts, and others), sequences—various illustrations that show different internal components of some object, and diagrams or schematic representations of how a machine functions where little three-dimensional representation is used.

Reconstructions

Many technical illustrations are imaginative compositions based on real data (an atlas, animal life, geology, space exploration, life of primitive humans, architectural reconstruction, and so on). These works usually require substantial documentation that can be

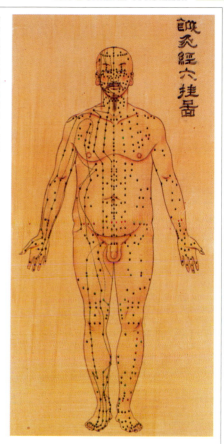

Illustrations such as this (a picture from oriental medicine) are the result of a detailed reconstruction based on comparative data. Illustration: Marcel Socias Studio.

brought together into a single image. The taste and the skill of the illustrator are entirely responsible for creating a whole that is clear, attractive, and faithful to all the aspects that the reconstruction brings together.

Reconstruction for a documentary book on animal life. Illustration by Antonio Muñoz.

THE DEMANDS OF REALISM

Every illustration that is conceived as a means of communication and information has to be more or less faithful to the reality pictured. In some cases, that faithfulness has to be extreme since the specific purpose of the work is to make some aspect of reality more comprehensible. Achieving realism in an illustration can be done in many ways, depending on the type of work for which it is intended. Each way is characterized by a special use of the graphic resources.

An Illustrator's Drawing

Skill in drawing is as important in illustration as it is in any technique in artistic painting. At various times, illustrations are based entirely on exactness and clarity in drawing, as with illustrations that are intended to be reproduced in black and white. No other aspect of technique can complement that type of illustration. The only feature that differentiates an illustrator's drawing from that of an actual artist is that the latter is not intended to be useful or put to a specific purpose, as illustrations are. Nevertheless, nowadays many examples

Alberto Durero, Aquilegia vulgaris. Albertina Library, Vienna (Austria). Scientific illustration can be tantamount to fine art.

George Stubbs, Anatomy of a Horse. The Royal Academy of Arts, London. The exactness and grace of this anatomical illustration has served as a model for many artists from the nineteenth century up to the present.

of illustrations can be found that are closer to contemporary art styles than to the rigid and objective representations of technical diagrams. Training for illustrators in the realm of drawing is no different from that of painters. They have to be familiar with the techniques of line and shading; they must be able to depict figures and objects both at rest and in movement; and they must have a fundamental knowledge of perspective and composition.

Pictorial Realism and Graphic Realism

Realism and pictorial elements in illustrations exist on different planes. In illustration, realism is a practical requirement, a medium for obtaining a result, whereas in painting, it is an artistic option, that is, it becomes a goal unto itself. Normally, rigorous realism is out of place in most illustrations for children, including many narrative illustrations. This type of work should focus more on the action than on detailed descriptions of objects. Just the same, for works in the technical and scientific realms, the utmost exactness is required in representing the details of an object, such as architectural and mechanical elements and botanical and anatomical illustrations, which have practical and informational purposes.

MORE ON THIS SUBJECT
• Changes in Scale and Tracings
  p. 60

Mastery of airbrush technique is one of the fundamentals of technical illustration.

Scale Drawings

In technical illustrations, making use of scale drawings done from photographs or plans is common. Reducing a drawing to scale can be quite laborious; exactness and minute detail are more important than artistic ability. Many illustrators project photographs onto the paper to create an image adjusted to the model as closely as possible. Nowadays, computer illustration has made calculating scales easier when producing the most complex technical illustrations.

Scale reproduction of the interior of a camera by Miquel Ferrón.

Techniques

Up to the present day, the airbrush has been the main feature of scientific and technical illustrations. Its rapidity and precision are unequaled by any other traditional method. The airbrush often produces results that, in terms of precision, are hard to distinguish from photographs.

Just the same, the computer has taken over the preferred place of the airbrush. Computers can produce results as precise as the airbrush can, they reduce the work required, and above all, they spare the artist from having to use the tools that go along with airbrush painting.

THE EDITORIAL PROCESS

The illustrator's work ends when the illustration is handed over to and approved by the client. The process that follows is the realm of the layout people, photoengravers, and printers. Just the same, the illustrator should know the route that the original will follow from the time it is delivered until it appears in the pages of a published book.

Layout

The layout person is charged with setting up the pages by arranging the paragraphs of text and the pictures, coordinating the sizes, evening out the pictures and the passages they illustrate, and being sure that everything conforms to the design criteria and is visually attractive. Usually, the pictures reach that person in the form of slides. They, and originals on paper (as long as they are of an appropriate size), are fed into a low-resolution scanner that digitizes them so that the illustrator can view them on a screen and adjust their size and appearance. Once the book has been laid out, the information is filed onto a magnetic disk, a zip disk, or a CD, and it is sent along with the transparencies and the originals to the photogravure shop.

The layout person places the pictures and the text onto the page and sends the montage, saved in a data-processing medium, to the photogravure shop.

The Precision Scanner

The scanner used by the layout person is very useful in organizing the material and placing it into the form in which it will appear when printed. However, it does not extract enough information from the pictures for the preparation of photolithographs; the results would be of very poor quality. That job is reserved for the high-resolution scanner. This is a very large machine whose top portion consists of a large, hollow glass cylinder to which the transparencies and originals are attached. When turned on, the cylinder spins at thousands of revolutions per minute while a laser reader (a small light on a movable arm) advances longitudinally to "read" the information contained in the transparencies or the opaque originals. This information is transmitted to a computer that captures it. Now the professional has the tools to place it into a spot previously occupied by the images in the

The graphics (originals and photos) are "read" by a high-resolution scanner, and this information is used in composing the illustrations for the final pages.

original layout. From that moment on, the design of the page is subjected to no more changes and is ready for addition of the photolithographs.

Photolithographs

Photolithographs are acetate films on which a version

Four pictures are made for each page; they correspond to the four colors of four-color printing.

Printing

In printing, each printing plate is inked with its corresponding color (magenta, cyan, yellow, or black). These plates are used to print the sheets of paper that will be the signatures that make up the book. Of course, the process requires the use of modern presses that work at high speeds and facilitate very precise adjustment of the proportions of each color based on the nature of the book.

of the page is produced in tiny black dots by a process very similar to photo developing. Four-color printing requires four of these films. One each is intended for cyan, magenta, yellow, or black ink (other films may be added in case a fifth color is to be included for special editions). These four films are superimposed and must form an exact reproduction of the page. Once it has been determined that no variation exists and that the films fit perfectly over one another, they are sent to a machine that transfers the information to aluminum plates engraved in relief by the paper impression, in other words, for the final production of the book.

The color films are used to produce the plates that will be used to print the work. Just the same, other machines produce the plates directly without using photolithographs: the CtP system.

ILLUSTRATING AS A PROFESSION

Many amateur artists exist who draw and paint for pleasure without seeking commercial outlets. However, all illustrators are professionals who get an economic return from their work. Clearly, illustrators choose their profession because of a natural disposition for drawing and painting. They always attempt to maintain their creativity in the face of demands from the marketplace.

The Context of Illustrating

In contrast with artists, illustrators function in a creative environment that depends on other professionals. Illustrations have to conform to a specific theme and often must observe certain technical specifications that define the work (size, process, surface, color, and so forth). In addition to the artistic work itself, a basic element of the profession is relating to art editors, the people who set the creative and commercial pace for the illustrator. For beginners, contacting the appropriate editors and getting some work published is very important even though the economic benefits will not be much at the start. Each original that gets published is a step ahead on one's personal career path, and it may open new doors.

Personalized Presentation

Before visiting editors who may be interested in the illustrator's work, sending information to all the eligible companies by way of personal introduction is a good idea. This introduction usually consists of color photocopies of the works, but sending cards or prints that present a more professional image of the illustrator's work is even better. The cards should have a certain amount of graphic originality in the typography and the general design or the inclusion of some image in order to distinguish them from

The Internet has many pages that function as a catalog of the work of many illustrators. Designing artistic Internet pages is a new avenue that has opened up for illustrators.

The work of illustrators is offered through image catalogs (right) published by agencies or in specialized books and magazines.

A good presentation for original works: the paper is protected against wrinkling and shielded by a thin sheet of tracing paper.

Graphic Design and Illustration

Graphic design and illustration move in separate but parallel realms in such a way that trends in one field always affect the other. That is a natural circumstance since both disciplines are destined to exist side by side on the same printed page. Illustrators need to know how to read the current trends not only in the illustrations produced for their colleagues but also in the characteristic aesthetics of graphic design, its typography, distribution of spaces, colors, and so forth. On the other hand, continually more illustrators use the computer and can manipulate images according to the parameters that make them perfectly compatible with modern graphic techniques and assure good reproduction.

MORE ON THIS SUBJECT

• The Editorial Process p. 24

the many that an editor keeps on file and that come from many different sources. In addition, a personalized card always suggests the artist's own creative style.

Aside from these cards, putting together a triptych or a pamphlet that reproduces a good selection of works and contains the artist's personal data may be a good idea.

Commercial Agreements

The issue of fees and honoraria is something that has to be worked out with each editor. Having some idea of what other illustrators charge is important so that the offer is reasonable. You have to remember that getting a commission for a single illustration is not the same as for a large number of them. In the latter case, the unit price will logically be lower than in the former. Just the same, when you are doing illustrations of varying complexity for the same client, the editor and illustrator usually agree on an average price per item.

A special folder for carrying and displaying originals, which are adequately protected in plastic sleeves.

ILLUSTRATIVE DRAWING

The profession of graphic illustrator, regardless of the artist's specialty or style, is built on drawing. Drawing is the graphic technique *par excellence*. Whether the illustration is realistic or not, mastery of drawing is a basic necessity for every illustrator. Every artist has a characteristic drawing style, either laborious or spontaneous, and it always has to capture the general idea or the subject of the illustration in a clear and effective manner.

Drawing Style

Typically, illustrators have to be multifaceted in their ability to depict all types of subjects. They also have to be ready to undertake commissions of very diverse kinds. As a result, they have to be very adaptable. Every type of illustration demands a drawing style. Illustrations for comics and graphic humor are based on a personal and free style. In contrast, technical illustrations require a very precise and standardized finish. The illustrator's spontaneous images are of paramount importance in illustrations for children. Generally, images designed to be painted require a somewhat simplified drawing, in contrast to ones in which line and form are the only technical resources.

No corrections are possible with brush drawing. A composition must be right the first time. Drawing by David Sanmiguel.

Surfaces for Drawing

Paper is the universal surface for drawing. Papers suited

Very detailed illustrations of complicated scenes demand lots of outlines and a sure talent for composition in sketching the figures. Sketch by Josep Torres.

The light and almost sketchy style of pen drawings demands great technical skill and total mastery of artistic drawing. Illustration by Vicenç Ballestar.

and fountain pens. Certain types of illustrations are done using strokes with an artist's brush and India ink. The technique required for this type of work, which is not used much today, is very refined since it requires controlling the stroke with greater or lesser hand pressure on the artist's brush.

The Human Body

Drawing is the basis for almost all types of illustration, and the basis for drawing is representation of the human body. This practice gives the illustrator the ability to depict practically any other subject adequately. All art schools consider drawing the human body to be a required course. In drawings of the human body, the illustrator's expertise is most clearly demonstrated.

to drawing with pencil have a slightly granular texture, while papers for drawing in ink have to have a smooth, hard surface. The smoother the surface, the better it is for producing precise lines. Grainy surfaces, on the other hand, produce more textured and imprecise strokes. This type of surface is used by artists whose work is very personalized and where textures and the decorative effects of blocks of color are important.

Many types of inks are used, from the traditional India ink (very opaque and satiny black) to colored inks. Different types of inks, both soluble and insoluble, are found in markers

Mediums for Drawing

The mediums used most frequently by illustrators are graphite pencils and ink. Graphite pencils are universal. They are easy to erase, and most professionals use them to sketch out the figures and objects of an illustration before coloring or inking it.

Computers will never be able to displace the traditional drawing skill required of an illustrator. Computer illustration by Toni Vidal.

ILLUSTRATIONS IN INK

Ink is the most traditional of the materials used by illustrators. The black, clear lines of an ink drawing facilitate reproduction and great precision in the work. Pen drawings are almost a specialty in themselves in the field of illustration. The widespread use of color in all types of printed mediums has diminished its importance a little since this type of drawing relies nearly exclusively on the use of India ink, which was the essential choice years ago.

Drawing with a Pen

Pen is a generic term that covers several techniques, including nibs, reeds, stylographic pens, pencil brushes, and fountain pens. Expert illustrators use these mediums without having to do a preliminary pencil sketch. At the most, they may use a pencil to sketch the basic lines of the work. Almost all the mediums mentioned respond immediately to the pressure exerted on them by varying the width of the line; this means that the line takes on an unmatched vitality that cannot be imitated by any other means. Other characteristics of ink drawings include the textures that can be created by shading, which runs the gamut from opaque black to transparent veils formed by cross-hatching. These drawing instruments require long practice to master their many possibilities.

Inks

All black inks tend to be called India ink. However, the many varieties are different for reasons of properties and color.

Real India ink is a very intense and slightly satiny black. Although insoluble in water once it has dried, India ink covers well, is opaque, and forms a solid and durable film on the paper. Other black inks have a slightly bluish or

One of the most traditional techniques of illustrating in ink involves using blocks of color: lines disappear, leaving black silhouettes to define forms. Work by Vicenç Ballestar.

Free and liberal application of ink using a pencil brush, reed, and nib yields very visual and satisfying results. Illustration by Vicenç Ballestar.

Reed is an excellent medium for illustrations that require detailed shading and clarity of line. Illustration by Francesc Llorens.

Fountain Pens

The fountain pen is the most modern of the utensils used for ink drawings. It works practically the same way as a modern fine-tipped marker except that fountain pens are made in very precise widths that always produce a uniform stroke (from 0.1 to 1 millimeter). They are customarily used in technical drawing or when the illustration will be painted and needs a perfectly visible outline.

are sometimes used to create spots of very intense, brilliant, and fairly transparent color. They are easily soluble in water, and they can be mixed with one another. Liquid watercolors and colored inks are not very stable in light, and they lose their color with time, so originals done with these substances have to be kept out of the light.

Drawing with Nibs and Reeds

When these utensils are used, the major feature of the drawing is the line that can be created by using nibs and reeds of different widths. Working nimbly and quickly is very important, varying the direction of the strokes and creating shading by accumulating lines. All lines done with nibs and reeds are clearly defined.

greenish cast and may be transparent and soluble after drying. These inks can be used in the manner of watercolors, in other words, by diluting them slightly with water to create thin layers of transparent tonality. Colored inks are very transparent and can be mixed with one another; their intensity can also be cut by adding a little water. When combined with black India ink, the effect has great visual impact. Similar to colored inks, liquid watercolors (also known as anilines)

Each of the tools used for ink drawings (nibs of different widths, reeds, and pencil brushes) produces a particular visual result.

ILLUSTRATIONS IN WATERCOLOR

Watercolor and gouache are the two graphic procedures most frequently used in illustration. Watercolors are a multifaceted technique that make possible a range from the most subtle and impressionistic coloration to the creation of bright and luminous works. Among the advantages that this technique offers are the possibilities of combining it with many other graphic processes.

Characteristics of Watercolor

Watercolors come in little containers or cups that contain tablets of semimoist colors that are quickly diluted by wetting them with a brush or else in tubes of creamy colors. However they come, watercolors are water soluble and transparent; their intensity depends on how much water is added to them. They mix perfectly with one another and have one essential advantage that distinguishes them from all other graphic procedures: The richness of tonalities depends not only on the mixes of the various colors but also on the amount of water added to the mixes. Since white does not exist (the underlying paper serves the purpose of the color white since the colors are trans-

Watercolor can be the simplest of all graphic mediums; it is ideal for attractive illustrations for children. Illustration by M. Àngels Comella.

parent), the colors lose none of their brilliance or their chromatic quality when they

Watercolors also allow for the creation of unexpected textures and effects that imitate other materials. Illustration by M. Àngels Comella.

are diluted with water. Watercolors dry quickly, and no solvents or other special substances are needed to use them. All you need is the colors, a container of water, and a brush.

Watercolor in Illustrations

In illustrating, watercolors are frequently used differently than with the traditional and truly pictorial manner of the artistic watercolorists. The latter usually emphasize brush strokes and patches of color, whereas illustrators use watercolors as a means of coloring and filling in shapes previously drawn with care. As a result, all watercolor illustrations begin with a well-executed drawing, usu-

With watercolors, the procedure always starts with very light and diluted patches of color.

Colors have to be darkened progressively, adding shadows to the clear, transparent areas.

Drying Times

Watercolors dry quite quickly (especially when papers or fairly smooth cardboards are used). If the area to be covered is fairly large, using broader brushes that make it possible to work quickly and keep the brush marks from showing is best.

If the illustrator needs the colors to stay wet for a longer time, a few drops of retardant can be added to the water. Ox bile is commonly used.

The pace of the work is dictated by the time needed for the colors to dry. The illustrator needs practice to become comfortable with this work rhythm.

ally done in light strokes with a fairly hard pencil. Coloring begins with the lighter tones sufficiently diluted with water, since diminishing the intensity of a color once it has been applied and allowed to dry is very difficult. All areas of the illustration are painted little by little by applying gradations of colors in the broad backgrounds. Gradations of color are cre-

ated by lightly moistening the area to be painted before applying the color and by extending the color little by little so that it blends with the water and progressively diminishes in intensity. After that, details can be added and colors can be intensified by superimposing layers of color onto the parts of

the illustration that have already dried. The colors lose a little of their vitality once they dry, and the illustrator can see if any retouching is needed only after the work is totally dry. In such cases, other graphic procedures may be used, such as gouache, colored pencils, pastels, and markers.

Watercolors allow for very finely tuned colors and richness of details. Illustration by Vicenç Ballestar.

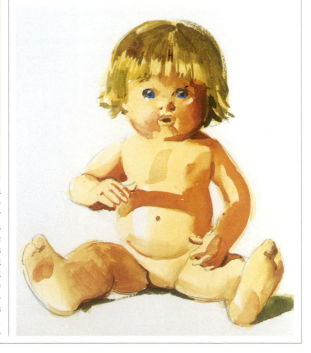

ILLUSTRATIONS IN GOUACHE

Gouache, like watercolor, is a water-based paint. The main difference is that gouache colors are opaque. This means that gouache is a less subtle medium than watercolors, but it has the advantage of allowing the artist to do all kinds of retouching and highlighting. Gouache makes it possible to create completely uniform areas of color. The tones are not lightened by transparency but rather by mixing with white.

Characteristics of Gouache

The finishes of illustrations done with gouache are uniform and velvety, and they can cover up any traces of brush strokes if the artist wishes. These characteristics make gouache an ideal medium for making posters in which areas of color are solid and clearly delineated. The reduced subtlety of gouache makes printing copies that remain faithful to the colors of the original easier. As a medium for retouching, gouache is practically irreplaceable in all kinds of illustrations, especially ones that require a highly refined finish and great detail.

Gouache colors are sold in tubes of soft color and in containers of somewhat thicker colors. Gouache colors sold in cups are of inferior quality that is acceptable for school children but not for much more. Manufacturers offer a broader range of gouache colors than watercolors. Since manufacturing quality opaque colors is easier than transparent colors, the companies can offer artists the precise colors they need for their works without having to mix other shades.

Technique and Procedure with Gouache

Hardly any difference exists between painting with gouache and with watercolors. The distinctive characteristic of gouache stems from the fact that the illustrator does not need to start with the lighter shades and gradually increase the intensity and darkness of the colors. Since gouache is opaque, it can be worked either from light

The appearance of cracking in this illustration is created by spreading gum arabic over the gouache once it is dry. Illustration by M. Àngels Comella.

Because gouache is easy to use, creating very striking visual effects is possible, as with the stenciling in this illustration by Montserrat Llongueras.

Transparencies in Gouache

If diluted using plenty of water, gouache colors can be used in transparent layers, although their tonalities are less delicately luminous than watercolors. Many artists use watercolors to create transparent backgrounds for works in gouache. However, once the opaque colors have been applied, they cannot be attenuated with successive transparent layers. This disadvantage is offset by the perfect uniformity and color saturation gouache offers; this is something that cannot be achieved with watercolors.

Works in gouache can be started either with light or with dark shades.

The visual characteristic of gouache relies on the opacity and the cleanliness of the patches of color.

to dark or dark to light. It accepts all types of highlighting and correcting. The colors are solid, but they also lighten somewhat in drying. That is why not using too much white to soften the tone is advisable since once the illustration is dry, it may appear floury and lack contrast. That is one reason why manufacturers offer such a variety of colors. By using them just as they come from the tube, the artist does not have to mix and use white to create colors. Retouching using gouache is very easy, and the result is scarcely visible in the finished work. Just as with watercolors, gouache illustrations can enrich and combine with other pictorial techniques, such as watercolors, markers, and colored pencils.

In contrast to watercolors, works done in gouache can be retouched with light colors to highlight the visual effect. Illustration by Jordi Homar.

ILLUSTRATING WITH COLORED PENCILS

The essential characteristic of colored pencils is the facility and the immediacy
with which they are used. They are manipulated just like a conventional pencil,
and they make possible a finish that is less greasy and more soft and satiny. They do not
require auxiliary mediums or any other equipment other than the pencils and the paper.

Small-Format Illustrations

This is a medium used to create small-format originals since the intensity of the shades and the covering capacity of the colors are much reduced in comparison to other mediums. The advantages associated with these factors include the possibility of incorporating a lot of detail in the illustration and the permanence and stability of the colors.

Colored pencils can be bought piecemeal. The large manufacturers sell many different sets that often come packaged in very elegant cases that hold from 12 to 140 colors. Some manufacturers offer pencils of different hardness (hard and soft; hard ones allow greater precision than the soft ones because putting a good point onto them

The appeal of colored pencils is not in saturated expanses of color but, rather, in the subtlety of colored lights and shading. Drawing by M. Angels Comella.

is easier) as well as others that are water soluble and can be used like watercolors. Recently, colored pencils have been introduced that

have thick leads more like pastels or waxes than traditional leads sheathed in a cedar shaft.

A colored pencil illustration always involves elaborating a good initial drawing.

Patches of color are created by accumulating superimposed strokes and achieving subtle colorations since using opaque, saturated masses of color is not possible.

Colored pencils demand delicate and detailed treatment that is not too pictorial. Illustration by David Sanmiguel.

colors. The pencils are a useful complement that can create, shade, and fill out forms previously painted in flat colors. This combination is practically traditional among artists, and it can be subsequently refined by touching up with gouache or pastels.

Combinations with Other Mediums

Colored pencils can be combined very easily with watercolors, and that combination yields the most subtle and delicate effects to be found in the field of illustration. With water-colorable pencils, this combination reaches a point where determining where one procedure leaves off and the other begins is impossible. Just the same, because of their limited covering capacity, colored pencils cannot be used in many pictorial mediums that are too energetic because they will not stand out enough.

Between Drawing and Painting

Colored pencil technique is halfway between drawing and painting. The intensity of the colors depends nearly as much on the pressure exerted onto the pencil point during the process as it does on the intensity of the color of the lead.

The colors are never as solid as those found in pastels, but large areas can be colored by using the side of the lead against the paper. The colors do not really mix, but they can be superimposed so that they create an effect of transparency. As a result, as with watercolors, the lighter colors have to be applied before the darker ones.

Strokes and Textures

One major resource available to artists who work with colored pencils is the texture of the paper. The rougher it is, the more visible the texture is in the finished work. Some artists use a lancet to score the surface before coloring

it in so that the pencil strokes will highlight the furrows and textures of the initial drawing. However, the most common use of colored pencils involves combining them with water-

MORE ON THIS SUBJECT

- Illustrative Drawing p. 28
- Procedures with Colored Pencils p. 72
- Techniques with Colored Pencils p. 74

Colored pencils can create excellent results on high-quality paper. Illustration by Miquel Ferrón.

ILLUSTRATING WITH MARKERS

Illustrators use markers as a means to create clean, well-matched colors; clear outlines; and a finished work that is easily reproducible by photomechanical means. Among all the pictorial mediums, markers offer the cleanest and crispest finish. They are used mainly in technical illustrations where sobriety and a certain precision are required.

Types of Ink

Most markers use water- or alcohol-based ink. Markers with water-based ink take longer to dry, and the colors mix when they are superimposed, even after they have dried. Some have opaque inks with a consistency very similar to that of gouache. It is effective in works that require solid blocks of color and uniform coverage. Just the same, the most commonly used markers have alcohol-based ink. This ink evaporates and dries quickly. Once it is dry, the color is indelible. Since it is transparent, colors can be applied on top of one another without mixing or running together. If the artist wants to produce shading and a finish free of visible strokes, the work has to be done quickly before the colors dry.

When markers are used on rough, colored surfaces (cork in this case), they produce some surprising effects. Illustration by M. Àngels Comella.

This delicate illustration by Jean Naudet shows the great subtlety of form and color that can be achieved by working with markers.

Graphic Designers and Interior Decorators

For a long time, markers were the medium most frequently used by graphic artists (for creating pasteups) and by interior designers to create an appearance as close as possible to the printed image. Currently, computer techniques have displaced this application for markers. However, the medium still holds interesting possibilities for creative illustrators who use them on textured surfaces and in combination with other techniques.

Markers are very useful for adding details to airbrush illustrations.

Fine Point and Broad Point

The point of the marker determines the appearance of the strokes and the blocks of color that are created. Conventional markers (for school use, for example) have a felt tip that produces a line of varying width that gets broader with use. Polyester points are much more durable and maintain a constant width. Markers with polyester tips are made in different sizes. The quality brands sell types that have two different points (fine and broad) on opposite ends of the same marker. Almost all the brands make markers with both fine and broad points. Professional illustrators customarily work in a very extensive spectrum of colors, and that keeps them from having to mix colors—always a difficult process in this medium. Every work dictates which colors must be used. When you buy markers, you have to remember that the color charts approximate the actual colors without duplicating them exactly. Therefore, before buying a marker, a good idea is to be sure of the exact color by trying it on a piece of white paper.

Mixed Techniques Using Markers

Sometimes, illustrations done with markers look much like watercolors, but markers cannot be used with so much freedom. The formats have to be smaller, and fewer blends are possible among colors. Just the same, markers can produce wonderful results in combination with other procedures, such as pastels, colored pencils, and watercolors. Also, the variety of surfaces that can be used with markers produces very different effects. Whether using conventional paper, watercolor paper, rice paper, silk paper containing fabric, or cork, the color and texture of the surface will remain visible and will impart a special character to the finished work.

Markers are frequently used in interior design and architectural design. Illustration by Helena de Canal.

ILLUSTRATING WITH PASTELS

Pastels are the closest thing to pure color without adding substances that are foreign to the pigments (the basic color substances that all pictorial mediums use). Pastels make possible creation of the deepest and most saturated colors. The colors are dense and velvety in nature. They need a fixative, a special aerosol lacquer that is sprayed over the finished work, to give it some durability.

Kinds of Pastels

Pastels can be either hard or soft. The former make it possible to work in greater detail than with the latter, but the soft pastels have better color quality because they are made with more pure pigment. Manufacturers offer boxes and sets of varying sizes as well as individual pieces. Most boxes combine hard and soft kinds in the same colors. One of the types most commonly used for illustration is pastel pencils; they look a lot like colored pencils, but they have a softer lead. Their advantage is in

Pastels produce decorative and textured results as well as realistic appearances. Illustration by Vicenç Ballestar.

Among drawing and painting, pastels enjoy the advantages of both procedures: freedom of stroke and density of color. Illustrations by Vicenç Ballestar.

Mixed Techniques

Pastels can be superimposed onto any type of surface painted with watercolors, gouache, or acrylic, provided that the layer of color is not too extensive (as with gouache and acrylic). This presumes painting on surfaces that do not have much texture and to which pastel does not adhere well. Some interesting results can also be created when pastels are used on wash drawings or washes of India or colored inks. Many illustrators work with pastels on very rough surfaces (wood, paper, fine grit sand paper, paper towel, plastered substrates, and so forth) in order to achieve rustic finishes that can take on the attractive appearance of aging.

Pastel can be used on different types of rough surfaces and may be combined with other mediums such as acrylic paint.

on the surface. This forces the particles of pigment into the paper and highlights its texture. Therefore, the grain of the paper is very important, and a wide variety of effects can be achieved according to the roughness of the surface. With pastels, shades of color are mixed directly on the surface by blending as described above, and they can be erased with a soft rubber eraser. Mixing colors is easy by working with colors in the same scale. Sets of colors are adequate for creating gradations from light to dark without having to use white or black but, rather, by working with pieces of slightly different shades. Pastels produce the best results in original works where the effects of texture are important.

their fine point, which makes it possible to work in minute detail.

Surfaces

Pastels can be used on any surface that is rough enough to hold the pigment when the pastel is rubbed onto it. Any watercolor paper is suitable for work with pastels, as are other drawing papers. One of the most commonly used for illustrations in general and for pastel pictures in particular is Canson cardboard, which is sold in a broad range of colors. Smooth surfaces are the only ones that do not take pastels well.

Techniques and Possibilities with Pastels

Techniques with pastels make it possible to work with lines or blocks of color. However, artists usually blend the two of them (according to the thickness of the lines) to create surfaces of velvety color whose texture coincides with that of the paper. The finger, a cotton ball, a piece of cloth, or a blender (a roll of soft paper twisted to a point) can be used to blend the strokes and patches of color

MORE ON THIS SUBJECT
• Procedures with Pastels p. 76

The grain or the texture of the surface determines the character of the finished work. This illustration was done by M. Àngels Comella on a highly textured surface.

ILLUSTRATIONS IN ACRYLICS

Among illustrators, acrylic paints have earned a place in airbrush techniques,
especially for illustrations that are rich in textures and original visual effects.
The possibilities of acrylic paints still offer a very broad field of exploration
for professional illustrators.

Characteristics of Acrylic Paints

A tremendous variety of acrylic paints exists in the marketplace. At every turn, new versions are introduced that increase the range of possibilities. The common denominator of all of them is quick drying time (acrylic paints dry as quickly as watercolors as long as they are not applied in too thick a layer),

MORE ON THIS SUBJECT

• Techniques with Acrylics p. 86

permanence of color, consistency in all types of atmospheric or light conditions, and impermeability. Once they are dry, acrylic colors are insoluble in water. They form an elastic and practically changeless film that resembles plastic. They are sold in tubes and cups of all sizes and shapes, and the range of colors is very broad.

Among the finishes available in stores are matte, glossy, iridescent, phosphorescent, and refracting shades in addition to substances that add body to the paste, make

Acrylic paint can be modified with various substances. This coarse texture was produced with an acrylic paste that contains mineral dust.

A wide range of possibilities, involving thicknesses, matte areas, smooth layers of color, and other components exists with acrylic paints. Illustration by David Sanmiguel.

The visual effect of illustrations done with acrylics can be created using visible brush strokes in certain areas, as in this work attributed to Almudena Carreño.

Acrylics make it possible to achieve results that range from the most strictly realistic to the most expressionistic and imaginative. They can be applied in perfectly smooth and uniform layers of color and in large blocks.

The fast drying time that characterizes these paints and the option of covering blocks of color with new, opaque shades make correcting and experimenting with colors as you go possible. In any case, as with all types of illustrations, working on the basis of a clearly conceived drawing is important.

Many illustrators use acrylics to imitate the finish of oil paintings without having to wait through the long drying times that oils involve.

The transparencies, the thicknesses, the textures, and the blending of colors that are characteristic of oils can be obtained with acrylic paints thanks to the great variety of additives that are available in the marketplace for this medium.

it more fluid, give it texture, reduce the gloss, make it more transparent, and accelerate or retard the drying. All these varieties are diluted with water. Acrylic colors are applied in essentially the same way as gouache.

Illustrating with Acrylic Colors

A large measure of the success obtained with acrylic paints in the field of illustration is due to the fact that they lend themselves to every imaginable type of finish: opaque, transparent, satin, textured, earthy, and so forth.

Combinations Using Acrylics

Acrylics can be combined with all the techniques that use water as an agglutinate as well as with dry techniques such as pastels and colored pencils. For mixed textures with acrylic colors, using enough water to make thin layers of paint is a good idea so that the other mediums are not entirely eclipsed by the body and energy of the acrylic paint. In any case, most artists use acrylics without combining them with other techniques since their intrinsic adaptability and the large number of accessory substances are adequate to create all imaginable effects of color, construction, consistency, and texture.

To give the paints a more earthy and rustic look, some illustrators mix conventional acrylic paints with powdered pigments.

ILLUSTRATIONS IN OILS

In oils, illustrators have sought and found a procedure for creating impeccably realistic representations. This is the very reason that oils have fallen somewhat into disuse for the purposes of illustration and have been supplanted by new technology. Nowadays, oils are used by illustrators who want finished works of high artistic quality similar to that of classical painting.

Characteristics of Oil Paints

Oil paints are composed of agglutinated pigments in linseed oil. They have a very creamy texture and an incomparable visual quality. A little color covers quite a large area. Oils can be diluted with essence of turpentine, essence of petroleum, or turpentine. Oils take a long time to dry, particularly when they are applied in thick layers. This makes touching up the work possible: the painter can modify the color or soften the shade hours or even days after applying it. Thanks to this

Working in oils requires using quite a number of utensils; it is a laborious and fairly slow technique.

quality of oil paints, artists can bring their works to the greatest possible level of realism and detail. Colors mix well with one another and can be blended in gradations of subtlety and complexity that are available with no other technique. Oil colors can be worked in transparency or in thick pastes. Many intermediate grades occur between these two possibilities. When diluted properly, oil paint can also be used with the airbrush technique.

Illustration by Yvan Viñals. Few illustrators use oils, but the ones who do always seek the greatest quality in construction and subtlety of color.

Frederic Remington, Cavalry Charge on the Southern Plains.
Between this illustration and an oil painting is merely a difference in style, not technique.

The Use of Oils in Illustration

Currently, oils used as a means of achieving maximum realism have been somewhat supplanted by procedures like airbrush and computer-assisted illustration. These produce vivid results and are less labor intensive. Just the same, oils are still used by the most demanding artists who seek a high level of artistic expression in their work.

Illustrating with Oil Paints

Illustrators who use oils do so to take maximum advantage of their realistic possibilities. The most attractive effects, in fact, come from attention to minute details. Oils permit all types of effects of transparency and texture. Certain kinds of substances modify their consistency, drying time, and the final appearance of the oil painting. However, they have a lesser effect on the basic procedure than in the case of other techniques such as painting with acrylics.

Oils and Other Mediums

The strong personality inherent to oil painting means that all the visual effects and resources it can produce come from the same procedure, and hardly any artists use unrelated techniques to create special effects. Oils can be combined with other oily mediums, such as waxes. They can also be applied over water-based colors such as acrylics and gouache, once the latter have dried. Some painters and illustrators begin their works with fine layers of gouache or pastels to check the effects of the color combinations before covering the entire work with oil paints.

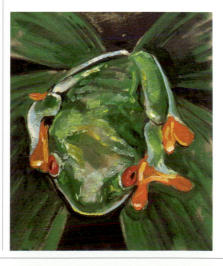

In this illustration by Miquel Ferrón, you can see the effects of transparency and texture that are possible with oils.

PROCEDURES AND MATERIALS

COLLAGES IN ILLUSTRATIONS

No other technique demonstrates more clearly than collage the intimate relationship between illustrative styles and creativeness. Collage was a contribution of the avant-garde artists at the start of the twentieth century (especially the cubists), and it had an immediate effect on all types of creative endeavor. Nowadays, many illustrators choose collage because of its immediate visual effect.

Materials and Tools

The basic principle of collage is the juxtaposition of surfaces of different color, texture, shape, and dimensions in order to create a visually interesting and suggestive ensemble. Based on this general assumption, the artist is free to use all kinds of papers to reach the goal.

The necessary tools include scissors, a hobbyist's knife, a metal ruler (used in conjunction with the knife), and some type of glue, depending on the size and the thickness of the papers to be used. The most frequently used glue is synthetic latex or white glue, which can be slightly diluted with water for delicate papers. Also needed are some natural-bristle pencil brushes in different sizes for applying the glue. They must all be washed immediately after use to keep the glue from hardening the bristles. Of course, having an abundance of all types of papers is necessary, including Canson-type colored drawing papers as well as wrapping papers and smooth, rough, cellulose, and rice papers, plus newsprint.

Color and Form in Collages

Even though the illustrator can color the papers used for making collages, a large part of the interest that this technique has involves taking advantage of the original colors of the materials used. That way, recognizing where the

Colored papers, cutting knives, glue, and so forth. These are the basic tools of the illustrator who works with collage.

cutouts came from at the same time that you appreciate the special configuration they have created is possible.

A uniformity of color is much more interesting if it is comprised of colored pieces from very diverse sources but

When cutting shapes out of paper, the color and the form are determined based on contrasts with neighboring shapes. The interplay between negative and positive, and between figures and background, remains the same.

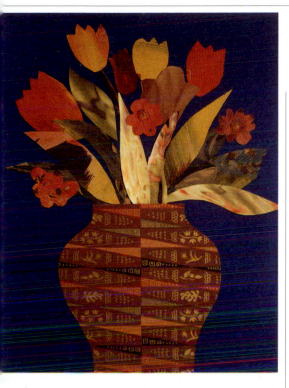

The interplay between surfaces and materials is an attractive addition to the simple juxtaposition of forms and colors in collage. Work by Anna Sadurní.

Surfaces

The larger the collage, the stiffer the surface should be and the thicker the cutouts should be. Using card stock or cardboard for mounting is usual (card-board for ink sketches is often used). For small col-lages made with cutouts from delicate papers, a thick paper or white card stock (or any other color that will go with the whole) will work. Deter-mining the compatibility of the glue and the sur-face so that the cutouts are firmly attached and do not come off easily is important. While they are working, some illus-trators use temporary glues that are easily re-moved and use perma-nent glues when they put together the final product.

which seem to participate in a common chain of discovery for the illustrator. The case is similar with the shapes, which must contrast among them-selves and retain similar-ties that avoid segregating the whole into disparate parts. The quality of the surfaces also plays a major role in the final appearance of the illustration; collage is more attractive if it presents contrasts in texture along with contrasts in shape and color.

In this work, the underlying surface is cardboard prepared with white paint, with colors applied on top. Using collages in illustrating does not involve a total abandonment of pictorial techniques. Work by Anna Sadurní.

THREE-DIMENSIONAL ILLUSTRATIONS

Even though pop-up illustrations date from antiquity, three-dimensional drawing is one of the most modern and enriching contributions of contemporary illustrating. Thanks to photographic reproduction, illustrators can create works based on relief figures using different materials than those traditionally found in drawing and painting.

Three-dimensional Illustrations

Three-dimensional illustrations are one more possibility among the many that modern reproduction techniques offer. The original turned in by the illustrator has to be photographed in order to produce the final product. As a result, the photographic quality is very important in this type of illustration, especially with regard to lighting since that is what makes the shapes stand out clearly. Illustrators can create the relief by using any type of materials that have body and rigidity, or else they can use very malleable materials (clay, Plasticine, plaster, and so on) that make creating relief that stands out clearly from the background

Colored card stock is the material most commonly used by illustrators who seek subtle effects of relief highlighted by gentle shadows. Work by David Sanmiguel.

possible. Trying to compile a definitive list of materials and possibilities involved with three-dimensional illustration would be futile, for scarcely any clearly delineated tendencies occur in a field governed almost exclusively by individual liberty of expression.

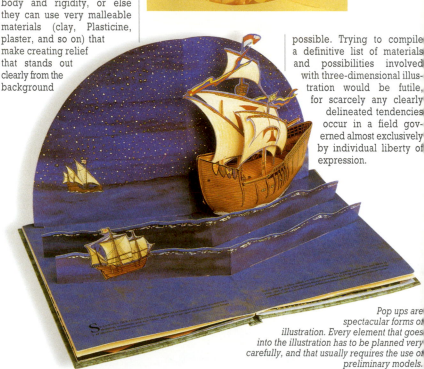

Pop ups are spectacular forms of illustration. Every element that goes into the illustration has to be planned very carefully, and that usually requires the use of preliminary models.

Three-dimensional illustration done in Plasticine by M. Àngels Comella. In this case, the Plasticine is used as a graphic material that creates its own shadows because of the relief.

Surfaces

Surfaces for three-dimensional illustrations need to be rigid and firm. They have to be prepared in the right way so that the various parts of the piece can be easily situated onto them. In some cases, using frames to hold together the assembly of parts that make up the illustration may be necessary. Anyway, the surface used for this type of illustration is rarely visible, and it is nothing more than a framework that is stable enough to hold the original.

Photographed Illustrations

The importance of the photographic technique in reproducing illustrations in three dimensions can assume a leading role in the creative process. The selection of objects, their placement, and the lighting that is brought to play on them is sometimes on the border that divides illustration from the photography studio. It is a borderland that modern professionals frequently visit. The results can be visually forceful and intense. From the viewpoint of form and color, they can be as creative as many other types of illustration.

Photographic illustration by the photographer Joan Soto. This is a wonderful collage of natural elements where everything has been carefully selected to achieve a decorative and realistic effect.

Pop Ups

Pop ups are illustrations that unfold in three dimensions and that are inserted into facing pages in a book. Pop ups stand up like a house of cards. When the book is closed, they fold up again. This type of illustration, except for in some books for children, is complicated to produce and somewhat costly from an editorial point of view. It is an uncommon type of commission for artists to receive.

Creating these pieces implies a close collaboration with the editors since the artist's creativity is influenced by the physical possibilities of making the piece work on a fixed budget.

The illustrator usually presents various models that clearly show how the work will unfold. These are made of papers of a similar or the same thickness as the ones that will be used in the book. Pop ups require quite a lot of ingenuity and manual and technical dexterity so that the flat surfaces move to create an interesting sense of volume.

PHOTOMONTAGE

Photomontage, more than a technique for illustrating, is a graphic product that can use all imaginable techniques. It is a contribution of the surrealistic creators. What started as a provocative experiment in visual arts has gained a foothold as one of the most attractive possibilities available to the professional illustrator.

David Sanmiguel: photomontage for a magazine. The surprising effects of which photomontage is capable have made it an appropriate vehicle for modern illustrations.

montage involves a very interesting and amusing creative process in which every solution gives rise to possible new graphic combinations.

Treatment of Images

In photomontage, pictures are the basic material that the illustrator uses. Any artist working in this genre of illustrating has a tremendous supply of images that can be used. They are gleaned from newspapers, magazines, catalogs, calendars, advertising, and other sources. The artist is practically condemned to keep every image that comes along because some day it may prove useful.

The best material comes from profusely illustrated magazines (fashion, interior design, news, specialty magazines, and so on) where the pictures can cover an

Image Play

Photomontage is a mix of visual techniques whose basic ingredients are photographic images and collage. However, even this broad definition does not encompass the entire area occupied by illustrations done with photomontage. When considering that reproductions of artistic works are also photographic images and that a photograph can be used as a detail as well as a colored shape, any printed image can be used as a component of photomontage. In addition, photo-

The combination of disparate images is one of the most interesting and attractive features of photomontage.

The combination of photographic images, cutouts, and painting is another option used by actual artists as well as graphic artists and illustrators. Photomontage by Ramón de Jesús.

entire page or even span two pages.

Currently, the high quality provided by color laser photocopiers allows the use of good reproductions of artistic works without damaging the books in which they are pictured. Color photocopies can be made of paintings and original drawings that no illustrator would use for raw material.

Materials

The materials that are commonly used for photomontage include paper or cardboard backgrounds, cutting implements (scissors and various hobbyist's knives), and glue.

Since photomontage involves creating originals based on the juxtaposition of disparate pieces, a major part of the work consists of cutting out the pictures. That is why

photomontage illustrators use hobbyist's knives with square and triangular blades for straight cuts, a scalpel-type knife with a curved blade for curved cuts, and knives with a pivoting head for straight and curved cuts that demand precision.

As for glue, using a removable aerosol adhesive that allows for gluing and separating the pieces of paper

as many times as may be necessary during the construction process and using permanent glues to attach the pieces in their final positions are common. In addition, markers and colored pencils may be used to touch up the pictures. The base for a photomontage may be thick paper, boxboard, or cardboard for montage.

As always, when working with hobbyist's knives, illustrators use a cutting board to protect the work table and preserve the cutting edge of the blades.

MORE ON THIS SUBJECT
- Collages in Illustrations p. 46
- Photomontage Process p. 63

Knives with heads that pivot are very useful for cutting out curved shapes very precisely.

THE AIRBRUSH

Since the development of color printing techniques, the airbrush has done more than any other mechanical tool to change the appearance of illustrations. The level of detail, the photographic finish, and the cleanliness of the finished works done with the airbrush were obtainable through no other means before the arrival of computer illustration.

Characteristics

Airbrush technique makes painting with a stream of pulverized liquid color similar to aerosols possible but with far greater precision. The stream is controlled by air pressure, the consistency of the paint, and the distance from the airbrush to the surface. The first of these factors can be controlled by several means, depending on the type of airbrush. The airbrush is basically a tube that ends in a small orifice that directs air pressurized by a compressor. As this air flows past a reservoir near the nozzle, it picks up color, pulverizes it, and transfers it to the surface. The control system for the airbrush consists of a button that regulates the passage of air.

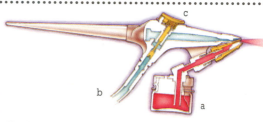

The airbrush makes spraying a mist of color from the reservoir possible (a) by means of compressed air introduced through a hose (b) connected to a compressor. The amounts of color and air are controlled by a button (c).

When the button is pressed, air is let into the body of the airbrush. It sucks the color out of the reservoir, mixes it with the air, and pulverizes it and expels it through the nozzle. The differences among airbrushes consist of the various systems to control the air pressure and the width of the paint stream.

The Mechanics of the Airbrush

Most airbrushes function in much the same way. All of them work on the same principle: a system for letting air in through a hose combined with the movement of a needle that opens and closes the orifice to the passage of the pulverized

The mist of color can be regulated for force (air pressure) and color intensity by moving the control lever in different directions.

Colors from the airbrush can be either opaque or transparent. The airbrush can create any number of effects, given the fact that the jet of color can be regulated.

color. The airbrush consists of a body with a valve through which air is admitted and a reservoir that contains the color.

In the case of gravity-fed airbrushes, where the reservoir is in the upper portion, the container may be part of the body of the airbrush or a cup. Inside this body, a sleeve protects the internal mechanism that contains the needle valve and makes using the tool possible. The upper part of the body of the airbrush contains the lever that controls the air and how much color is picked up.

In one type of airbrush, the color reservoir is located on one side or below the body. This type offers the advantage of holding a lot more color than gravity-fed airbrushes; reservoirs with different colors can be changed quickly and easily washed. On the other hand, they are bulkier and less well-balanced than gravity-fed airbrushes. They also do not afford quite the same freedom of movement.

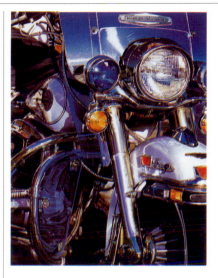

Superrealistic work by Hideaki Kodama. The results of careful and detailed work with an airbrush have a visual brilliance that cannot be achieved with any other process.

Colors

Airbrush paints can be either opaque or transparent. The choice of one or the other determines the appearance of the finished product. Opaque colors are solid shades appropriate to works where clarity of detail is crucial. Transparent colors facilitate very subtle visual effects. They also work very well with the photographic effects that characterize airbrush technique. All the paints have to be liquid or soluble in water or some other solvent. Paints that contain large particles in suspension should be avoided for they can clog the airbrush.

Illustration and Experimental Art

Nowadays, the airbrush is fully accepted in the world of illustration and fine arts. It is used by commercial artists as well as avant-garde experimental artists. For the former, it is an indispensable tool for creating high-resolution pictures, retouching photographs, and creating advertising images. For the latter, it is a medium that holds new possibilities. Alone or in combination with other procedures, it brings graphic creation into new territory.

Illustration by Philip Colier. The airbrush is one of the most valuable allies that ad illustrators have.

COMPUTER ILLUSTRATIONS

The profession of illustrating has not sat on the sidelines in recent years during the computer revolution. Computers are being used with greater frequency to create and manipulate all kinds of images. In large measure, they have shown themselves to be strong competitors of systems such as the airbrush. This technology is in constant evolution. It will not replace traditional mediums, but it has already opened up new areas and styles.

Equipment

Everything connected to computers is subject to a dizzying process of change and innovation. Novelties become old hat in the course of a couple of months, and the equipment is constantly increasing in capabilities. Inevitably, once this book reaches readers, the market-place will already offer new features that will surpass the possibilities of the machines mentioned here. Still, the general orientation and the use of the programs will be sub-stantially the same. The best working conditions with a truly effective program for dealing with images can be had only with a high-capacity machine. An adequate machine should have about 200 MB of RAM, 30 GB of hard-drive memory, and an 800 MHz processor. Although some illustrators work with a graphic palette (a flat surface used with a pointer), many continue to work with a conventional mouse; familiarity with the tool is more important than its theoretical level of precision.

Basic Options

The general window of the program is the surface on which the illustrator works, somewhat like paper or canvas for a painter. Ruled frames are at the top and the left; both rules permit setting or modify-ing the dimensions of the il-lustration. As with any other type of computer program, the *Photoshop* program for hand-ling images (the one used most frequently by profes-

Size of the Work

Every computer illustration has a set size, resolution, and weight. The programs have options for adjust-ing all these parameters that allow for setting or modifying the size of the image and its resolution. These two factors deter-mine the weight of the image, that is, the amount of computer memory that the picture takes up.

sionals) has a menu bar at the top of the screen that contains the options *File*, *Edit*, and *Image* (for selecting size, posi-tion, color treatment, and so forth), *Layer* (for creating, ad-ding, removing, viewing, and combining layers), *Filter* (for effects of texture, color, focus, distortion, and others), and the more conventional *View*, *Window*, and *Help*, in addi-tion to the drop-down windows that appear when you select one of these options with the pointer.

Professional equipment needs to have lots of memory and a fast processor that responds nimbly to the pace of the illustrator's work.

Program tool bar. Most of these functions (line draw, color, airbrush effects, select pieces, gradations, and so on) have other functions that multiply the possibilities.

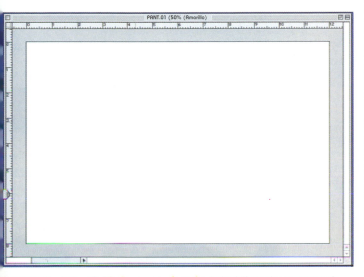

The general window of a blank program where the desired illustration appears and from which all the tools of the floating tool bar are activated.

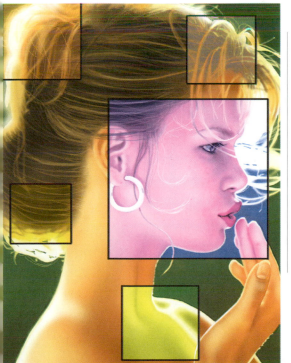

Programs

Programs are available on the market for drawing and handling images: vectorial programs and bitmaps. The former makes possible the creation of lighter images that take up much less memory, but they do not allow for altering their resolution. That means that they lose some quality when they are enlarged.

The program most frequently used by professionals is *Adobe Photoshop* in its various versions. Its use is similar to airbrush, and the results are of the highest quality and precision.

An image is comprised of different layers of color. This picture shows various windows where different features of the image appear without one or more of these layers.

DOCUMENTATION

A large number of illustrations require documentation, in other words, graphic models from which to extract the necessary information. These models can be photographs, sketches, or other illustrations. All professional artists have a file containing an assortment of this type of material. Sometimes it is provided by the editor who commissions the work.

Sources of Documentation

The type of documentation that an illustrator uses is determined by the nature of the work. Doing an illustration for a children's book is one thing, one done entirely for a scientific publication is another. In any case, the level of rigor will be dictated by the editor. The editor can provide necessary documentation to the illustrator if needed. Many illustrators frequent secondhand bookstores where they get illustrated books on the broadest range of topics that are not available in conventional bookstores: works on clothing, catalogs of old engravings, period illustrations, old

Many illustrations require searching for enough graphic material to cover the documentary needs of the job.

Sometimes the illustrator will have to take pictures to get the needed documentation.

Variety in Documentation

In many cases, going to more than one source to find the necessary documentary information is necessary. In a historical reconstruction, for example, the illustration can be done based only on partial information (clothing, landscape, architecture, and others) that the artist has to interpret and blend into the work. When other illustrations are used for documentation, using more than one documentary source to avoid plagiarism is necessary. An artist's work always has to be original.

Sometimes what seem to be the simplest parts of an illustration make creating photographic documentation necessary.

to the next. Each illustrator files and stores magazines, individual images, cutouts, and photocopies in a different way, usually according to subject in folders or filing cabinets.

Graphic and Written Documentation

The type of documentation most useful to the illustrator is, of course, graphic in nature: sketches, photographs, other illustrations, and so forth. With narrative illustrations, maintaining strict faithfulness to the events of the story, and especially to the characterization of the people, is extremely important. The character imagined by the illustrator may never meet all the reader's expectations since every reader, and the illustrator as well, imagines the characters differently. However, the illustrator's creation will be accepted as long as it adheres to all the details expressed in the narrative. As a result, the written documentation must be respected at least as much as the graphic documentation, especially when it is the only source of information available to the illustrator.

magazines, and so on. These works contain very valuable information for artists, not only because of the images they contain, but also because of the style of illustration that may suggest new approaches. In exceptional cases, illustrators may, in fact, be required to do their own documentation by going to the site and taking pictures or notes.

A Personal File

As time goes on, every illustrator accumulates a personal picture file as well as a reference library. These libraries contain classics or useful books recognized by all artists. These collections are created and expanded according to the needs of the illustrator, so they may vary tremendously from one artist

Illustrators do not use only printed documentation; scale models are very useful for some types of work.

TECHNIQUES AND PRACTICES

MODELS

Models are the first graphic approximation of any project. Like the plans for a building, every new publication is first presented in model form: a book with text and imagined pictures that give an overall idea of the appearance that the finished publication will have. In many cases, the illustrator has to adapt to a previous pasteup or even propose to the editor a pasteup of the page in which the illustration will be inserted.

Balance Between the Text and Image

When the illustrator has to present a pasteup for a publication, as with some works for children, the main thing to consider is the balance between text and pictures.

Typically, the editor determines the parameters of those proportions. The illustrator's job is to distribute the appropriate images in various formats (half page, full page, or double page). The distribution of illustrations throughout a narrative work has to be such that it does not interfere with the flow of the reading experience. There must not

MORE ON THIS SUBJECT

• Documentation p. 56

be too much separation between the episode illustrated and the corresponding picture. There must be a balance in sequencing the images so that they provide a general idea of the plot independently of the text.

It is usually up to the graphic designer to create a good balance between text and pictures. That is why the illustrator's proposal usually has to pass muster with the designer before it gets a green light.

Adjusting the Illustration

Most of the time, illustrators do not have to concern themselves with adapting their work to some editorial plan, but sometimes the editor provides a detailed pasteup into which the illustration must fit. This happens, for example, in the case of decorative illustrations—ones that accompany and complement some part of a text and that are more of a visual complement to the general design than a graphic representation of the work's content. In such cases, the illustrator has to adjust the shape and size of the illustration to the requirements of the

Here is a pasteup done by the illustrator, using a simulated text, that facilitates checking the general effect of the illustration on the page.

XXX XXXXXX
XXXXXX

Xxxx xx xxxxxxxx xxxxxx xxxx xxxx xxxxxxx xxx xxx xxxx x xxxxxx xxxx xxxx xx xxxxxxxx xxxxxx xxxx xxxx x xxxxxx xxxxxx xx xxxxx xxxxxxxx xxxx xxxx xx- xxxxx xxx xxx xxxx x xxxxxx

Before doing an illustration, preparing a pasteup of the most important pages of the publication is sometimes necessary to get the pictures and the text adjusted just right.

Questions of Size

The illustrator usually works on a considerably larger scale than the final size of the work on the printed page. That makes sense. Producing the details of an illustration while working in a larger format is easier. Once it is reproduced in a smaller size, the illustration increases in quality since it appears far more minute and richer in details than it really is. This general rule is subject to exceptions when the final size of the reproduction is either very small or much larger than the original.

An illustration designed to be printed very small does not allow for very much detail, for it would appear mottled and confused. Conversely, when the reproduction is very large, the original can be done in comparable dimensions.

page carefully. A similar case exists when the illustration is of a technical nature and contains fillets with explanations, sketches, and additional details (for example, an anatomical illustration broken down into several parts). The pasteup has to be planned very carefully to avoid compromising the clarity and legibility of the page.

Many illustrations require a series of sketches and initial attempts in addition to pasteups in order to assure proper adjustment of the original to the requirements of the job.

CHANGES IN SCALE AND TRACINGS

When illustrators work on the basis of detailed sketches or photographs,
making tracings to function as a basic drawing for the illustration is common.
The original photograph or picture is not always the right size. In order to adjust
the size while conserving the features of the original picture, an illustrator
uses different methods for changing the scale.

Light Table

The easiest way to do a tracing is to use a light table. This is a flat box whose upper surface is white translucent glass, or plastic. Inside the box are several neon bulbs. When the bulbs are turned on, the surface of the box is flooded with light. Any opaque picture (photographs, drawings, and others) can be put onto it for tracing with onto equally opaque paper, as long as the papers are not too thick.

A light table is a box containing neon bulbs that makes tracing original pictures easy.

The greater the illuminating power of the light table, the thicker the paper can be, since the light passes through the original picture as well as the surface and the first is visible through the second. This is exactly the same principle as tracing on a well-illuminated windowpane, except that the light table provides much more light and it is more even and completely white. Light tables come in many different sizes, and they are not difficult to make with a little bit of skill and patience.

The strength of the neon bulbs makes tracing pictures easy when working with fairly thick papers.

Grids

Using a grid is a more traditional way of enlarging original pictures. It consists of drawing an even grid onto the original. If you want to copy the original in the same dimensions, you have to create a grid on the paper exactly equal to the one imposed on the original. On the other hand, if the intent is to create an enlargement, the grid on the drawing paper has to be larger, not in terms of the number of squares, but in terms of their size. For ex-

Grids are the most precise method of expanding the scale of a picture for subsequent use in an illustration.

In addition to conventional slide projectors, there are also projectors for opaque originals, such as this one, that make working with drawings and photographs possible.

very sizable dimensions. The only drawback is that every enlargement produces small distortions, in addition to the understandable loss of definition. This can create some serious problems in works that demand exactness of scale.

A projector is a great help when you have to work in large scale and you do not need much definition in the shapes.

ample, if each square in the original is 2 inches (5 cm) on a side, the expanded grid could measure 2.75 inches (7 cm) per side. The grid makes it easy to copy all the details of the original exactly and keep the proportions just right.

Enlargements

Reprographic enlargements (enlarged photocopies) are the easiest and most commonly used means of adjusting the size of an original photograph to the desired illustration. Nowadays, the quality of black-and-white and color copies is excellent, and the copies can be made quite large. Illustrators can put together partial enlargements to create an enlargement of

SURFACES

Each process requires a particular type of surface that matches the nature of the medium and allows the artist to work conveniently. The most frequently used surface is paper in all its variations, but other surfaces include fabric, cardboard, and prepared woods.

Paper

Paper is the universal surface for nearly all originals since it is adapted to all types of techniques, with but few exceptions. Paper or boxboard is the only appropriate surface for procedures such as pen and ink, watercolor, gouache, and colored pencils. Ink requires a smooth or satiny paper on which the nib, the brush, or the cane can glide easily. Watercolor and gouache require a thicker paper that has more body and absorption. The thin lines of colored pencils that do not offer much coverage do not show up on surfaces that are textured or darker than conventional white paper. In addition, if they are used on very grainy papers, more texture is in the finished work, but including lots of details or creating patches of dense color is not possible. That is

Rigid and fairly stiff surfaces (cardboard, wood, and fabric) can be used with such techniques as gouache, acrylic, and oil paint as long as the surface in question has been treated with a preparatory coat.

why professionals usually choose smooth or untextured papers. Originals done with colored pencils are usually of small dimensions. In large illustrations, colored pencils are typically used only as an auxiliary technique.

Porous Surfaces

Markers can be used on practically any porous surface, including impermeable ones such as plastic or glass, if the markers are permanent ones. The porosity of the surface should not be excessive.

Paper is the most commonly used surface for all types of illustrations. Smooth, satin, rough, or highly textured, every paper has its application and is appropriate for a specific procedure.

Some surfaces that are useful for painting with oils, acrylics, gouache, and mixed techniques. From left to right: fabrics treated with transparent and opaque sealers, woods, and cardboards.

With papers that are too spongy, the point of the marker could catch and immediately deposit excess ink. The usual surfaces are smooth or satin papers, rice papers, and acetates, which are composed of a stiff plastic emulsion.

Surfaces for Acrylic Paints

Acrylic paints can be applied to any type of surface except those with a slick or very satiny finish. The best surfaces are slightly absorbent, such as boxboard and cardboard, treated fabrics, sealed woods, smooth paper, and so forth. All brands of acrylic colors also offer paints with a white colored base known as *gesso;* it is used to prepare surfaces that are too absorbent.

Cardboard for Mounting

Mounting cardboard or mat board is used mostly for displaying original works. It is light, stiff, and easy to cut. Illustrators who work in photomontage and collage often use it to keep glued pieces from wrinkling or coming loose because of movement in the underlying surface.

Surfaces for Oil Paints

The universal surface for oil paints is cotton or linen canvas or linen treated with a white sealer and stretched over a wooden frame. Many artists use boards covered with canvas or prepared with a special sealing paste for oil paints. Cardboard and papers that have been properly sealed so that the oil is not absorbed too quickly can also be used.

Gesso is the universal preparation for fabrics, cardboards, and woods. It is a white paste that is spread over the surface and that is compatible with nearly all mediums.

PROCEDURES WITH WATERCOLORS

Procedures with watercolors and gouache are similar in their initial stages, but they are considerably different in their finishes. Watercolor is a more subtle medium that requires more delicacy than gouache. Since gouache is a more graphic medium, it can be applied more directly and energetically.

Transparency and Opacity

The transparency of water-colors requires starting any project with lighter shades and advancing toward darker ones through successive layers. Many illustrators apply a highly diluted initial base coat onto which the shapes are painted in somewhat darker colors. Watercolors make creating subtle and con-tinuous gradations possible by working on the moistened paper. That makes it an ideal process for depicting atmospheric effects and for smoothly modeling large vol-umes such as terrain, land-scape features, and other large compositional masses. The opacity of gouache makes it a more direct technique, and it

Watercolors are easy to spread out and make it possible to cover large areas of color gradations that act as backgrounds.

can be used to start filling in more solid and intense colors right away.

Possibilities with Watercolors

The inherent nature of watercolors and the possibili-ties of applying them to dif-ferent surfaces and in com-bination with other techniques make them appealing to illus-trators. They explore the pos-sibilities of their medium at least as much as artistic paint-ers and attempt to extract from it all the possibilities that have any visual appeal. The possibilities of watercolors become evident in conceptual and decorative illustrations that do not require the artist to do a literal representation of

Watercolors are the ideal medium for illustrations that require clarity of design and simple and attractive color, as demonstrated in this illustration by Montserrat Tobella.

the object depicted. Some of the effects that can be achieved using watercolors include splashes, spots, drips, scratch patterns, and abstract blotches, whether textured or not. Almost all of them make maximum use of the essential virtue of watercolors: their transparency. To these variations can also be added the many different qualities that can be obtained by selecting different papers.

Compatibility with Other Techniques

Watercolors are compatible with all drawing techniques (especially pen and ink, pastels, and colored pencils) and, of course, with gouache. The traditional combination used by many illustrators involves touching up areas of watercolor with colored pencils to create fine shading and details that are hard to achieve with a brush. Because of its delicacy, the watercolor

is always used first. The other processes mentioned—plus many more that the

artist may discover through graphic experimentation—can be applied on top of that.

Lines, Blocks of Color, and Details

The great adaptability of watercolors fosters all kinds of illustrative styles. They can be used to draw colored lines with the tip of the brush or with contrasting areas of color that create color planes. Just the same, most illustrators use them for details, accumulating small and precise touches that constitute the image, and focusing attention on the intensity and coloration of each area or background of color.

Watercolor illustration by Roman Hennel.

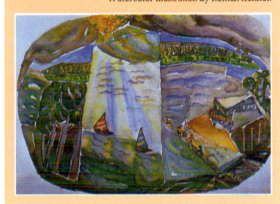

Watercolor can be a very precise technique. Highly detailed works can be created by using very fine pencil brushes.

Mixed techniques using watercolors can include such unpredictable materials as waxes. Illustration by M. Àngels Comella.

WATERCOLOR TECHNIQUE

These pictures show the usual way a watercolor illustration is created and the reasons behind the series of stages that the artist follows to create a clear and attractive image with a sports theme. The main qualities of this work are transparency of color, richness of shades, and subtlety of mixes.

Areas of Color and Reserves

Before being painted, the illustration has to be drawn perfectly in pencil. Using a pencil with a hard lead is best to create light and precise lines that will not be visible once the work is completed. As with most graphic procedures, a watercolor illustration advances from the general to the specific, from the large areas of color to the small details. Therefore, for the initial background colors to match the final background colors is logical.

Color Gradations

One of the basic resources that watercolors offer is the possibility of creating areas of color gradations with a single application of paint (using a single brush stroke). This can be done so that the colored area has integrity, without recourse to touching up or highlighting. This is the resource that is commonly used to create backgrounds that will set off the main subject of the illustration.

The first stage of a watercolor illustration shows a balance of light and transparent shades. The human figure is the focus of the work, and it has been outlined for subsequent elaboration.

The blank figure in reserve is first covered with a wash of transparent, highly diluted color that will serve as the color base for subsequent applications.

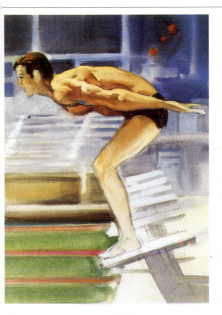

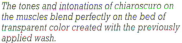

The tones and intonations of chiaroscuro on the muscles blend perfectly on the bed of transparent color created with the previously applied wash.

Here one can see how the background is further elaborated in parallel with the human figure; areas previously painted are touched up to maintain the contrast and the unity of the entire illustration.

Modeling

Modeling the figure concentrates the interest in the work. This modeling is produced by first applying a very diluted coat of color to create the general chromatic base of the body.

On top of this base of color, darker shades are added to correspond to soft shadows. After that, the darkest areas are accentuated to set off the relief in the muscles.

The entire body, both its light and dark areas, must be worked in the same color range to present visual unity.

Details

Once the figure has been outlined definitively, all the necessary details can be introduced, according to the type of illustration. Maintaining a balance between these details and the whole is crucial so that too many details do not interfere with the integrity of the illustration and diminish its visual impact. Retouching should be kept to a minimum to avoid overloading the areas of color and spoiling their transparency and freshness.

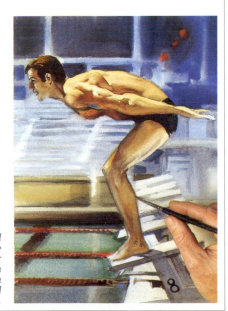

Details and outlines have to be saved for the end, when the illustration is in its final form.

PROCEDURES WITH GOUACHE

Gouache does not permit as much subtlety as watercolors, but it does offer greater power of color and an opacity that makes it ideal for graphic art. It is very simple to use. It does not require as much planning as watercolors since the colors can be superimposed and they cover one another effectively.

Possibilities with Gouache

Since this is a more solid and dense technique than watercolors, gouache allows for a more energetic and resolute treatment. It can also be used in conjunction with many other materials and techniques. Because they are opaque, gouache colors are commonly used for all types of illustrations, to superimpose details or areas of color, create textures, outline areas of color, create stippling, or simply reinforce certain areas by adding new shades. The density of gouache colors makes it possible to imitate the textures and finishes of acrylic paints (for which they can be substituted in most

Depending on the tool used to apply it, the color can present distinctive textures, as in this illustration by M. Àngels Comella, in which the color was applied with a sponge.

Different applications of color (using a sponge, a brush, and so on) produce intriguing, contrasting effects. Gouache illustration by M. Àngels Comella.

instances) and even oils. Still, one has to be careful not to make thick impastos—thick layers of color—with gouache for they tend to crack and come off the paper. While speaking of such things, never roll up a paper that has been painted with gouache, even originals painted in thin layers. To assure the permanence and good preservation of the works, a good idea is to work on rigid surfaces or mount illustrations done on paper onto a thick piece of cardboard.

MORE ON THIS SUBJECT
• Ilustrations in Gouache p. 34

Gouache also allows for precise and very graphic results, as in this illustration by Myriam Ferrón.

Adding Gum Arbic

Gum arabic is the agglutinating substance in gouache that ties the pigments together and gives it fluidity. Creating effects of aging or cracking is possible by apply-ing a layer of gum arabic on the original fi-nish. If gum arabic is added to the color while it is being wor-ked, the color becomes more fluid and transparent. How-ever, the colors lose solidity, and controlling the areas of co-lor becomes difficult. Illustrators must experiment in advance to produce the desired effects.

Compatibility with Other Techniques

Gouache can be combined with any other type of artistic technique except oil. Oil can be applied to a gouache base, but the reverse is not feasible. Gouache does provide the most spectacular results when used on unconventional surfaces such as wood, plastic, and even aluminum foil. Some works done on unusual surfaces may have very little longevity (especially ones on nonporous surfaces, to which gouache does not adhere very well), but they can last long enough to be photographed for publication.

Dry-Brush Technique

Dry-brush technique consists of painting with a brush loaded with plenty of color that is not very dilute so that the lines are irregular and reveal the texture of the paper. Achieving the thick color when working with watercolors is hard, and that is why this technique is typically used with gouache. Dry-brush painting is one typical way of creating textures in gouache illustrations when the work is already quite far along.

Applying opaque touches of color over dried, previously covered areas creates an irregular chromatic patina that can imitate qualities such as stone. Working directly with a dry brush, with no previous preparation, is also possible. The result is sketchy and energetic, and it presents the rustic appearance of an illustration done with elementary materials.

The opacity and the homogeneity of gouache colors make them particularly well suited to illustrations where color is the major decorative element.

GOUACHE TECHNIQUE

Gouache has lots in common with watercolors. Both procedures are based on dissolving the colors in water and working with large patches of color. Just the same, gouache colors are much more solid and opaque than watercolors. So in gouache illustrations, the artist can create interplays and contrasts between transparent and opaque areas.

Coloring in General

General coloring in a gouache illustration is not much different from in a water-color. In both cases, you apply color well dissolved in water. With gouache, the colors are not transparent and luminous as with watercolors. That is not a problem, though, because the illustrator can cover broad areas of the work with great ease.

Once the drawing is done, the background of the illustration is colored with gouache washes using brush strokes that suggest the movement of the water.

This is only one of many possible resources with gouache: splattering paint onto the illustration to simulate drops of water.

As with watercolor illustrations, large patches of color have to harmonize with the main theme of the composition as defined by an exact sketch done with a hard pencil. In the example that illustrates these pages, the spray from the water occupies the majority of the work. Its effect is created by spreading out the wash of color with series of brush strokes.

Effects of Splattering

Because of their greater opacity, gouache colors can be manipulated to create a broad spectrum of effects. That is the case with the splatters from an artist's brush or a toothbrush. This consists of loading a dry artist's brush

The modeling of the figure is less subtle with gouache than with watercolors; it starts with dark patches that set up the shaded areas of the flesh.

made with stiff natural bristles or a toothbrush with thick paint and then rubbing the finger over the bristles to splatter the paint onto the illustration. This is just one of the many effects that are possible with gouache; these effects must always be justified by the nature of the subject. In this case, the splatters create an effective representation of the drops that dot the curtain of water created by the skier.

Modeling and Details

When the background is filled in enough, the figure is worked starting with the lightest shades, with the most dilute color, until the figure takes on a preliminary volume. This first modeling consists of painting the darker flesh tones and leaving the illuminated sections white. Gouache does not allow such subtle effects as does watercolor, and the contrasts between light and dark are neater and clearer. Modeling is accomplished by seeking intermediate values between the darker and lighter flesh tones and creating a continuous transition from one to the other without sharp demarcations.

The rest of the flesh tones and colors of the figure are painted using flat colors but without modeling.

The final touches involve details that can be added using paints directly and without mixing.

The finished illustration by Myriam Ferrón shows the appeal and the lively color that can be created with gouache paints.

PROCEDURES WITH COLORED PENCILS

When compared with other drawing techniques, working with colored pencils is small-scale work. Pencils do not facilitate working in large formats. They produce their best results when they are used for details rather than the large, plastic effects that charcoal, pastel, or paint require. This limitation also creates the technique's interest and undeniable charm since it demands an attentive, delicate, and sensitive treatment.

Lines and Color

Drawing with colored pencils also amounts to coloring. The appearance of the color consequently depends on the type of stroke that is used. Muted colors are created using lines that are crossed yet separated in space so that they do not cover the paper entirely. The accumulation of lines can be quick and free or premeditated in the form of superimposed diagonal cross-hatching. This works well when a unified color is desired. When you draw with pencils, the colors will never be very saturated, but you can cover larger areas by using the side of the pencil lead against the paper.

Lines play a crucial role in illustrations done with colored pencil. Work by Joaquim Chavarría.

MORE ON THIS SUBJECT

- Illustrating with Colored Pencils p. 36
- Techniques with Colored Pencils p. 74

Mixing Colors

More than mixing, this really involves superimposing colors since a physical mixture is not possible. The colors that result from superimposing

Colored pencils produce excellent results for both realistic and decorative illustrations. Work by Joaquim Chavarría.

different shades of colored pencils are governed by the theory of color. The primary colors yellow, blue, and red produce the secondary colors orange (yellow and red), green (yellow and blue), and purple (red and blue). Illustrators always use a broad range of colors—precisely so they do not have to mix—including both primary and secondary ones. However, it is a rare illustration that does not demand superimposing two colors to create a third. These superpositions have

In small-scale illustrations, pencils allow for great precision and excellent color density.

Drawing by Ramón de Jesús. The white of the paper can fulfill an important task in illustrations done with colored pencils.

do be done in a specific order: the light color has to be applied over the dark one. That is because the light colors do not cover as well and they let the base color show through—which is needed to create the desired color. If, for example, a red is applied on top of a yellow, the resulting color will be the same red slightly tinted with orange. On the other hand, if the yellow is put on over the red, the orange will show up clearly.

Fusing Colors

Colored pencils have one property that is peculiar to them and due to their physical makeup. This is the possibility of blending lines of light gray or white onto another color. The somewhat waxy consistency of the lead is stronger than the scant coloring power of the white or gray shades. It makes the lines blend with one another without being affected by the gray or the white. Some shades not only blend with one another but hide one another when they are covered by the gray. This is a very useful resource for all types of works done in colored pencil.

Water-Colorable Pencils

Water-colorable pencils offer new possibilities for mixing that can be added to the typical superposition of this technique. This involves a true mixture of pigments produced by dissolving the colors in water. When these pencils are used, the mixtures are not created separately on a palette but right on the paper after applying the colors in such a way that the water blends the lines and produces the desired hue.

This colored pencil work by M. Pilar Navarro shows simplicity and sensitivity.

TECHNIQUES WITH COLORED PENCILS

The sequence illustrated on these pages shows the usual way in which illustrators who use colored pencils work. This is a simple process that requires clear composition in advance and considerable delicacy in coloring and shading the figures represented.

The Importance of the Grain of the Paper

The smoothness of the paper is a crucial factor in working with colored pencils. The smoother the surface, the more subtle and detailed the illustration can be. That is why professionals always use smooth paper when they do very detailed and realistic works. Papers with a heavy or grainy texture, though, make the lines stand out more. However, they do not permit dense coloring since the texture of the surface is always clearly visible in the final result.

Layout and Details

Line drawing in illustrations always has to be careful and precise, especially when colored pencils are used. These are a type of colored drawing rather than painting. As a result, almost all the work consists of drawing and modeling the shapes using lines. Once the outline of each object has been established, the color is applied, making as few corrections as possible, since the limited covering capacity of colored pencils would make corrections visible. The colored pencil lines are precisely what are used to establish the

The preliminary sketch must be done in a neutral color or one that belongs to the dominant scale used for the subject.

shapes and the details of the subject with the greatest clarity. For the preliminary layout, using neutral colors that do not have anything to do with the subsequent coloring (grays, ochers, or siennas) is common. The lines should be firm and continuous, without hesitation.

Coloring

Coloring an illustration done with colored pencils involves progressively accumulating lines so that in the early stages, the shades are always much softer than at the end. This allows the illustrator to check the color balance at any

Coloring is methodical and progressive; it begins with light lines and advances toward more solid colors.

MORE ON THE SUBJECT

• Illustrating with Colored Pencils
  p. 36

Colored pencils need to be quite sharp for creating details.

Finishes

The delicacy and attractiveness of the colored-pencil technique are clearly seen in the finished illustration.

The fine point of the pencils—extremely fine when they are well sharpened—makes possible the creation of very tiny details. Perhaps even more interestingly, they permit carefully crafted shadings and shapes, representations of shines, folds, and all types of chromatic hues that delicately enrich the illustration.

time and darken the shades wherever necessary. The reverse is not possible for colored pencils can scarcely be lightened by using white. Additionally, erasing does not work well since that leaves a visible mark in the completed illustration. The gradation of chiaroscuro, that is, the modeling of the objects, is easily accomplished by using intermediary colors between the lighted and shaded areas of each object and blending them all with delicate, superimposed strokes.

Finally, the background areas are colored in and the color contrasts in the illustration are reinforced.

This example shows the process of adjusting the hues with colored pencils. First an area is lightly covered with color.

The second color has to be applied with more force but without covering the first one entirely. The result is not a true mixture but a combination of two colors that influence one another.

PROCEDURES WITH PASTELS

Pastels and colored pencils entail no technical complexities, and their use is as direct as the act of drawing. Colored pencils are a means of retouching all types of illustrations. When used by themselves, they provide subtle qualities and delicate coloration. More energetic than colored pencils are pastels, a medium that offers greater visual force.

Pencils and Hard Pastels

Most pastel artists do an outline of their work using strokes of one of the colors that will contribute to the harmony of the overall illustration. Still, charcoal could be used as long as you consider the effect it will produce on the colors when they are blended in with the initial strokes. Pastel pencils are the logical medium for doing colored drawings and lines, outlines, and details in the paintings. The strokes created with pastel pencils are somewhat thicker than with conventional pencils, but pastel pencils can be sharpened fairly well as long as care is taken to avoid breaking the fragile points.

Sticks of hard pastel are very useful in works that incorporate light coloring based especially on linear and graphic grace. The edges of square, hard pastels are very helpful in drawing straight lines. By holding the edge of a stick against the paper and moving it horizontally, you can produce very precise straight lines. The same can be done with soft pastels, except that the line produced will, of course, be a bit thicker.

MORE ON THIS SUBJECT

- Illustrating with Colored Pencils p. 36
- Illustrating with Pastels p. 40
- Surfaces p. 62

The first stage of a work done using hard pastels. These show the texture of the paper much more clearly than soft pastels do.

Hard pastels do not cover as effectively as the soft ones do, but they produce interesting effects of texture. Illustration by Miquel Ferrón.

Coloring with Soft Pastels

Soft pastels make it possible to cover large areas with saturated color that are much more intense than what can be accomplished with pastel sticks. Just the same, they produce broad strokes, and they cannot be used to create details, especially when the original is of small dimensions. When working with soft pastels, using a free and pictorial style composed of generous areas and large superpositions of color is typical. This means that soft pastels are rarely used for detailed works, or ones that require clear and precise lines, unless they are used to color in a background on which other mediums will be used.

Soft pastels provide lots of color intensity and are very easy to blend.

The Issue of Fixing Pastels

All traditional manuals categorically advise against using fixatives on pastel works. Currently, the marketplace provides artists with very high-quality fixatives. They are aerosols that anchor the pigment to the paper, that do not smudge the colors, and that produce matte finishes in accordance with the nature of the procedure. So fixatives can be applied to pastels without problem. The reason that traditional manuals discourage the use of fixatives is that they alter the relationships between colors. They saturate and slightly obscure the shades and sometimes destroy the freshness of the lines. That is true, especially if many coats of fixative are applied. The solution to the problem consists of applying a very fine coat of fixative and then correcting any colors that may appear to be altered. Another solution involves fixing the different layers of color as the work progresses and leaving the last one without fixative.

In contrast to colored pencils, pastels cover well, and they can be used over colors applied previously.

PROCEDURES WITH MARKERS

Markers make possible the creation of both sketchy works and very precise drawings with a perfect finish. Water-colorable markers may be the best suited to the latter possibility. They incorporate lines and blocks of color. They can also be used spontaneously, allowing the lines to run freely and then filling in the patches with color.

When used on very granular paper, markers produce an interesting and rustic finish. Work by M. Àngels Comella.

Techniques with Markers

Working with markers is similar to working with colored pencils, but some important differences need to be pointed out. In the first place, the initial drawing of the outlines should be done with the right color for each of the shapes depicted. If a generic color such as a gray is used for the preliminary drawing, this color may distort the final effect in some light colored areas where it may remain too visible—unless a sketchy and free effect is desired and these factors are of no consequence. Therefore, the initial sketch is done in colors. Following a sequence from light to dark is also a good idea since light shades do not cover dark ones. The shade of the

Blocks of Color and Mixes

Fine-tipped markers, the best kind for drawing, are a medium that allows for precise definition of contours as well as effects of color and shading. Like colored pencils, markers can be superimposed onto one another using lines or blocks of fairly solid color. In general, not many mixtures are possible with markers unless they are water colorable and can be diluted with a brush and water. Even in that case, the dark colors overpower the light ones in mixes.

The illustrator has to keep that factor in mind in searching for precise shades by mixing two or more colors. Also, markers are used quite quickly and the strokes are fairly broad since they pro-

duce lines of saturated color without having to press down on the point.

In technical works, an illustration done with markers has to be very carefully planned and precise in perspective.

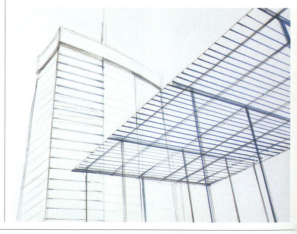

markers is independent of the intensity of the stroke. As a result, each color can produce just one intensity. Sufficiently broad ranges of color are needed to allow for different shades within each color. The best results are obtained when several shades of each color range are used for areas of a similar hue.

Direct Mixes and Mixes Using Gray

Direct color mixes involve superimposing strokes of one color on top of another. This technique works fine when dealing with colors in the same spectrum or when the idea is to darken one color. It is not effective when a homogeneous mixture is desired, that is, a mixture in which the two superimposed colors produce a pure third color. Direct mixtures should not be used at the

When working on a solid linear structure, markers make possible the creation of technical illustrations with great freshness of color.

start of the procedure because they tend to darken and sully the hues while the illustration is being worked on. As with colored pencils, marker lines can be mixed almost until they disappear by rubbing them with light gray or any light color from the set plus gray. When gray is applied on top of another color, it unifies the hues and blends the outlines, thereby slightly attenuating the rather garish appearance of a polychrome illustration.

Water-Colorable Markers

As with water-colorable pencils, markers with soluble ink can produce results similar to watercolors. Still, marker inks are much more intense, less transparent, and less suitable for wash effects. Dilutions can only be local. Applying too much water in attempting to spread out the color is not a good idea. You have to work in small areas, blending and diluting the various hues. Also not advisable is to blend to the point where the lines are eliminated, because that defeats the very technique of drawing with markers.

Work by M. Àngels Comella using water-colorable markers.

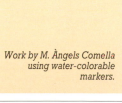

PROCEDURES WITH INK

When ink is used for drawing, it makes possible many different treatments depending on the instrument used to apply it. The nib is the most common one, but reeds, artist's brushes, and conventional writing pens can all be used. Depending on the choice, the results can vary from the most meticulous and detailed to spontaneous effects of spots, washes, graphics, and others.

Nibs

Writing ink is one of the cleanest and most direct mediums. The fineness of the lines makes it possible to work in smaller formats than with any other procedure. At the same time, it makes creating large-scale works harder.

In drawing with any kind of pen or nib, the line is much finer than normal in other drawing procedures. It is also more permanent. In drawing with ink, no room is available for trial runs intended to be erased or hidden by other thicker and bolder lines. In short, lines done in ink require greater certainty. The breadth of the ink line is essentially constant. This width does not depend, as it does in other procedures, on the pressure exerted on the point. Rather, it is related to

By using their flat face, nibs make drawing broad and irregular lines possible.

the type and to the point of the nib or reed used. In the case of nibs, the line is of consistent width. It cannot be varied, regardless of the amount of ink used, unless the point

is pressed onto the paper to the point of separating, at which point the nib drains quickly.

Reeds

Lines made with reeds allow for certain variation, depending on which side of the point is applied to the paper. In working with the reed held like a stylographic pen, the line is broad and continuous, with minor variations possible in response to the pressure used. Using the side of the point produces a finer line (around half the width of the usual line made by the reed) that is less stable. The combination of fine and broad lines can also be alternated with another possibility that is peculiar and exclusive to reeds: blended lines, or ones that do not fully cover and are

Reeds produce lively and varied lines, but they are a little more demanding to control than conventional pens.

Permanence of Ink

While India ink is very permanent and stable, colored inks eventually fade in prolonged exposure to light. Sooner or later, an original done in colored inks will lose its color. So keeping it in a box, away from any source of light, is a good idea.

Nibs and stylographs are used primarily for technical illustrations and other works that demand great precision.

faint due to a lack of ink. Whereas nibs cease to mark all of a sudden when they exhaust their supply of ink, reeds make lines that become progressively lighter. The illustrator can take advantage of that to create certain effects. These effects are often medium-intensity shading created by an accumulation of parallel strokes that do not cover entirely, sketched outlines, and transitions between one clear area and another area darkened by opaque lines.

Colored Inks

Drawing with colored inks is comparable to drawing with India ink, except it requires working in a certain order. Even though inks can be mixed with one another, the results are not always very attractive since they tend to sully one another and turn out somewhat cloudy. The only truly viable mixtures are ones produced by a combination of different colored strokes on the paper. To maintain cleanliness during the procedure, using at least two nibs is a good idea, one each for dark and light colors. Both nibs can be inserted alternatively in a single holder.

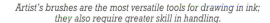

Artist's brushes are the most versatile tools for drawing in ink; they also require greater skill in handling.

TECHNIQUES FOR PEN DRAWINGS

Drawing with a pen is one of the oldest specialties of the genre. India ink
has its own qualities that make it attractive, whether it is worked with
nibs or reeds. The following sequence will show how a pen-and-ink
illustration is done. Instead of using a traditional nib, a modern pen with a built-in ink
reservoir will be used.

Lines of Different Widths

Drawing pens with an ink reservoir are very useful tools for creating black-and-white illustrations where no major contrasts in lines are required. Pens with ink reservoirs do not allow for a line that is as sensitive to hand pressure as with a conventional nib. However, this factor is compensated for by its convenience of use since it is used just like a conventional stylographic pen.

Just the same, it should be pointed out that pens with built-in reservoirs allow for two types of lines: fine and coarse. The fine line is produced by drawing on the paper with the point upside down. When the pen is held normally, it produces the broader line. These two possibilities are adequate for creating different visual effects, combining small patches

In order to be sure that the image fits the format and is properly proportioned in all of its parts, it is first done as a preliminary sketch and then gone over in ink.

with fine and coarse lines, applied in different densities and shaded lightly or heavily.

Developing the Work

Whenever you work with India ink, you have to do a light, preliminary pencil sketch to be sure that the proportions are right and the figures are placed correctly onto the pa-

per. Then this sketch is gone over and elaborated by adding the necessary details. In this illustration, the outline is gone over in a continuous line of even width. In some details, though, such as the mane on the zebra's neck, you can see some light lines done with the point turned over. The contrast in line widths is important in creating a truly graphic effect in this type of work.

Working with the back of the nib produces finer lines that make possible the creation of opaque blacks, as on the animal's muzzle.

After carefully outlining the stripes on the head, they are filled in with opaque black.

Silhouettes

Cross-hatching is a basic resource for illustrators who use India ink applied with nibs. This consists of more or less dense networks of lines that cross one another to form blocks of light and shadow. It has great visual impact that recalls the traditional technique of acid engraving. The breadth of the line and the density of the cross-hatching determine the texture of the shadows. They offer great versatility in value from the white of the paper to the most dense and opaque blacks, including all kinds of intermediate shades produced by intersections between straight and curved lines.

Pen-and-ink illustration by Joan Sabater.

Contrasts

The pure contrast between black and white is the graphic value par excellence and the reason that pen-and-ink illustrations are so effective. Nevertheless, the simple contrast between completely white areas and patches of black lacks appeal: you have to add shadows and intermediate values created through parallel or crossing lines in order to create more subtlety and interest in the work.

In the sequence, you can see how the stripes of the zebra's coat set up the basic black-and-white contrast. The subtle strokes used in the shading of the mane and the muzzle lighten and provide variety to the alternation between black-and-white areas.

In order to achieve an interesting appearance in the mane, you have to alternate quick, fine strokes and broad ones.

Finally, some light shadows are superimposed onto the black areas that make up the zebra's stripes.

PROCEDURES WITH ACRYLIC PAINTS

Acrylic paints, which are used as a fairly conventional means of coloring,
are very easy to use. If soft brushes are used (typically composed of synthetic bristles),
all the necessary layers can be superimposed by accumulating fine films of
transparent or opaque colors. Acrylic paints dry very quickly and allow
the artist to make the work really stand out.

In works conceived in flat colors, the areas of color have to be clearly established right from the outset.

to be prepared before painting with one or two coats of primer (commercially known as gesso). Dried gesso can be sanded smooth enough so that the paint flows smoothly on it and can be worked in transparent layers. If acrylic paints are used on paper that has not been prepared, they dry more quickly than usual, and that makes creating effects of transparency almost impossible. As a re-

The good covering capacity of acrylics makes them very well suited to works with rich, dense coloration and great clarity and graphic legibility. Work by Almudena Carreño.

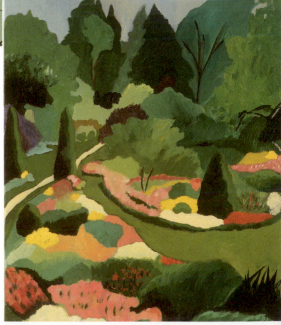

Choosing the Right Surface

Acrylic paints can be approached like a procedure that is halfway between oils and watercolors, with the delicacy of the latter and the covering qualities of the former. Painters normally choose canvas. However, most illustrators prefer paper or prepared cardboard because these mediums are easier to transport and present. In general, papers and cardboards have

The heavy, creamy colors of acrylics create a particular graphic quality. Work by M. Braunstein.

Acrylics are also used as a means of coloring templates. In this picture, you can see how a cardboard template is constructed.

sult, the smoother the surface, the greater the transparency and the luminosity of the coloration.

First Steps

The initial sketch is usually done in soft pencil, which will not affect the color as charcoal might. The drawing should simply be done in outlines, with no shading or additional tracing. The color will fill in these lines, and there is no point in cluttering up the sketch.

The first patches of color should be even shades without cuts (like the ones in watercolors when the color dries on the paper before spreading it out completely), applied in layers of color substantially diluted with water. In the places where the color is too dark, a little water can be applied to even it out. Conversely, if the color is too light in some places, more will have to be added.

Once the backgrounds have been painted, the procedure involves adjusting the shades by adding successive layers of color in opaque or transparent films in order to create the appearance of volume. Waiting for the first layers to dry before painting any subsequent ones is a good idea unless the illustrator wants the colors to mix on the paper. Once the sense of volume has been achieved, the work can be elaborated by creating effects of texture: grooves, lumps, and thick areas of paint that lend variety to the illustration.

MORE ON THIS SUBJECT

· Illustrations in Acrylics p. 42

Acrylics on Textured Surfaces

Many illustrators choose to work on the surfaces of their originals before painting them in order to create effects and qualities that cannot be created by painting alone.

These effects are created by such things as making grooves or scratches in the prime coat (the coat of gesso), leaving some areas rough and smoothing others with sandpaper, and impressing the pattern of coarse cloth into the wet primer. Working in this way implies prior and certain knowledge of the effect that each measure will produce on the base coat.

TECHNIQUES WITH ACRYLICS

Acrylic paints produce results very similar to those of oils when they are used
in realistic illustrations worked in the traditional manner using colored
shapes, shading, impasto, and so forth. The following procedure
is an example of one realistic possibility of acrylic paints
used for illustrating.

General Applications

As with oil painting, when working with acrylics, covering the entire surface with patches of color, starting with the first phases of the work, is very important. This serves to confirm that there is a balance in the general color composition of the work and that the parts fit properly into the whole.

With oils, these areas of color are usually filled in using very dilute colors. Since acrylic paints are much more transparent when they are diluted, applying them in thicker layers is a good idea. Of course, all the colored areas must coincide with the forms delineated in the preliminary sketch.

When observing the procedure for illustrating shown on these pages, the lower part of the composition, which corresponds to the ice, requires a lighter coat than the rest. The color should not be too solid here in order to suggest the transparency of the hues of the ice.

Because acrylic paints dry quickly, they make possible the use of dense colors for the initial blocking.

The forms are worked with plenty of paste since no danger exists of their mixing with the base coat, which has already dried.

Flat Applications

Diametrically opposed to realistic illustration is the flat treatment of the image based on the visual contrast among a restricted number of inks or between these inks and the white of the paper. Acrylic colors also have good potential in this regard since they can be used like dense gouache colors that cover well and dry quickly.

Illustration by Ramón de Jesús.

The color blocking provides a very precise image of the subject in nearly all its details.

The tiniest details can be applied with a very fine pencil brush, toning and refining without any danger that the small lines and details will mix with the base color.

Modeling

Since acrylic paints dry quickly, they make it possible to work on the shapes almost immediately after applying the first color blocks. No need exists, as it does with oils, to increase the density and the consistency of the colors in stages. The different dark and light gradations of each color can be done using dense brush strokes in different shades. In the case of figures clearly silhouetted against a very dark background, the contrasting effect is strong enough so that the figures can be modeled softly.

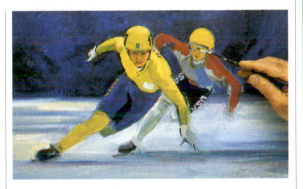

Details

The final details of the figures (for example, faces and details on clothing) are added at the end using a fine artist's brush and working on top of the dried paint. Once again, the rapid drying of acrylic paints works to the advantage of the final detailing. The fine lines and color blocks applied with fairly fluid paint flow onto the base coat of paint without mixing with it, and they create vivid contrasts and hues. Finally, the surface of the ice is gone over with fine strokes and lines in different tones of white, gray, and black to create a faithful representation of its texture.

MORE ON THIS SUBJECT
• Illustrations in Acrylics p. 42

The result is a realistic illustration that has a lot in common with works done in oils.

COLLAGE TECHNIQUE

There are as many collage techniques as there are artists who use the medium: collages using colored papers, painted papers, remnants, woods, cardboards, combinations of materials, and so forth. This sequence shows collage technique combined with painting. It conserves the visual freshness of the mixed pieces and the density and the quality of the subject of the illustration.

General Design

The general design of the work should always be very simple. An excess of complexity and details in the conception makes the work harder to create, and above all, the result lacks spontaneity. Therefore, the preliminary drawing should be schematic and orientational so that it gives free rein to spontaneity and improvisation in the later stages of the project.

This sequence shows the creation of a still life: a table on which are a tablecloth and a series of objects. The preliminary sketch, which was done with charcoal, is very rudimentary. It merely serves to determine the position of each object.

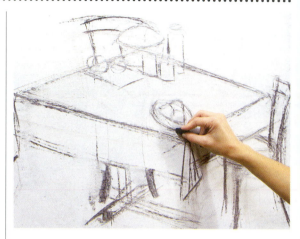

The preliminary sketch for a collage should be very simple. It need not be any more elaborate than a general sketch.

MORE ON THIS SUBJECT
• Collages in Illustrations p. 46

Selecting Papers

Papers are chosen according to their thickness and color. Using a limited palette of colors is a good idea so that the finished product has a harmonious color scheme. Too much contrast always produces confusing and garish results. The variety of papers runs from the finest to fairly

Before gluing the cutouts into place, check their position by using a removable adhesive.

Once the cutouts have been checked for effect, they can be anchored into place with permanent glue.

thick watercolor papers. One of the best papers for use in collage is wrapping paper, which is sold in various colors, all of which go well with one another. Once the papers are chosen, they are cut out in accordance with the size and shape of the area to be covered. They are glued into place with an appropriate adhesive; white glue is the most common choice.

Gluing

Many illustrators use two types of adhesive: a light, removable one that is easy to pull apart and another that is permanent. First, they check the fit of the cutouts by positioning them with the help of the removable adhesive. If they like the effect, they glue the piece down for good with the permanent glue. In the work illustrated here, the effect created by the papers is combined with several coats of texture (white acrylic paint mixed with sand) in order to highlight the contrasts between surfaces. The construction of the

When calculating the size and orientation of each cutout, it is placed onto the work and carefully trimmed with a hobbyist's knife.

The finished work by Ester Serra is remarkable for its careful contrast between the different glued and painted surfaces.

Combining Textures

Combining textures is the key to most collages. Different textures may result from the thickness of the cutouts or from the surfaces. In addition, the artist can change the texture of the paper or cardboard cutouts by applying thick paint on which grooves and different granulation effects can be created.

Illustration by Ramón de Jesús.

work progresses through stages involving form, color, and texture.

Different Surfaces

The objective is to keep the work from turning into a conglomeration of different types of surfaces. It should be a unified whole made interesting by diverse contrasts in shape, material, and color. Achieving this will require experimenting with different papers to come up with the right combination. The final phase of the work consists of applying the final textures with paint in order to fill up the hollows left by the different paper cutouts.

AIRBRUSH TECHNIQUE

As an important example of airbrush technique, here is how a human figure can
be painted without reference to a photograph. This requires using all kinds of
masks, both fixed and movable, as well as several technical resources
that provide an overview of the array of graphic possibilities
that the airbrush offers.

Advertising Illustrations

Precision in the initial drawing is essential when working from photographs and even more so when working from a sketch or from notes. In this case, creating a highly detailed drawing is essential because the masks will have to be cut out with absolute precision for every area to be kept in reserve. As a result, the drawing involves planning for all the necessary masks.

Masks

Clouds can be masked with cotton. Loose cotton threads are stuck to the surface with tiny pieces of adhesive tape or with rubber cement. Thanks to the texture of the cotton, the spray filters between the fibers and produces a good gradation that is almost

Transparencies, Shines, and Sparkles

By combining sprays, highlighting with opaque colors, and using masks very carefully, impeccably realistic effects can be created that are impossible to produce with any other technique. As with transparencies, shines and sparkles are quite easy to produce using an airbrush. These sparkles are, in fact, derived from a photographic vision in which light is trapped for an instant. The airbrush can capture this type of realistic, photographic appearance better than any other medium.

*The photographic effects are among
the most interesting advantages of
working with airbrushing.*

*All the contours of the drawing have to
be perfectly defined.*

*The masks are cut out to coincide with the areas
established in the preliminary drawing.*

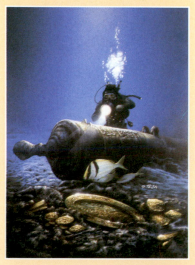

impossible to imitate when working freehand and without masking. For the blue mountains in the background, you can use a movable mask made from torn paper. The figure is likewise masked when the background of the landscape is painted. After that is painted, it is masked in turn while a general spray is applied to create the base of flesh tones for the figure. Once that is done, the remainder of the work involves using different types of movable masking, retouching, and reserves of white.

The Head and Hair

Self-sticking masks must be used for the head of the figure. They are placed around the hair and leave it exposed. Before spraying, liquid glue is used to create a series of curved lines that represent the sheen of the hair. Next, the entire area is covered with color, and the mask is removed with an art gum eraser. To create the shading in the tufts of hair, a mask can be cut out of thin cardboard with slits of different length and breadth in a half-moon shape and alternated with different sprays to create the desired effect.

Movable masks such as this thin cardboard cutout can be used to facilitate painting the hair.

Another movable mask: a template of curves makes it easy to create the fruit.

Reserves and Templates

The still life in the foreground must be held in reserve throughout the process since it requires a different treatment. In the first place, everything that is not part of the still life is reserved with a self-sticking mask. The seeds of the watermelon are painted by hand, and the surrounding area is carefully sprayed to create the effect of texture. The fruits can be created with the help of oval and circular templates. The glass and the cocktail shaker incorporate shines and reflections.

The finished work by Miquel Ferrón, in which various types of masks and typical airbrush techniques were used.

COMPUTER TECHNIQUES (I)

Some professionals use a scanner to capture photographs and paint on them to create a finish similar to what can be obtained with an airbrush. Others prefer to draw and color each illustration as if they were using traditional implements, first drawing and then coloring. This way of working produces more personalized and less conventionally photographic results. However, it requires a high level of skill in drawing and lots of practice and dexterity with the mouse.

First Layers

The point of departure is a freehand drawing based on a photograph. This is the first layer of the work. The line corresponds to a size 2 on the airbrush with 100 percent pressure and in a dark color other than black—a kind of sepia chosen from the normal palette. Drawing the lines of the illustration by hand has created closed areas that can be selected individually. The selection tool is the *magic wand*, and the coloring of the work begins by selecting the face area. In airbrush terms, this selection is the equivalent of cutting out the center of a mask to uncover the area of the face and neck and then performing a similar procedure with the hand.

Flesh Tones

The painting is accomplished by using different diameters of "spray" (which range between values of 30 and 200) with a very light pressure (12 percent) to avoid creating excessively dark spots. The colors were created by combining cyan, yellow, magenta, and black. Once these colors are identified, they are incorporated into the palette to be used throughout the work session. These are toasted hues (flesh tones) of different intensity. This painting constitutes a second layer. Little by little, the details are put into place, working with different thicknesses, smooth-

Even though the mouse is used, this is still a freehand drawing that requires all the skills of an artist.

ing the color transitions with intermediate hues, creating details with very fine strokes,

and superimposing lines of different colors to represent the blond hairs of the figure.

Once the layers have been selected, each one is worked with all the precision and subtlety that the computer program allows.

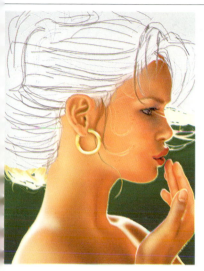

Flesh tones have a visual quality that is difficult to reproduce with any other method.

Assembling the Layers

When the work is completed and it is clear that the illustration has been done properly, the layers have to be assembled and saved as a whole. Once that is done, the illustration can no longer be separated into its component parts. It can be retouched only by adding new layers, manipulating the color parameters, adding filters for special effects, and adjusting the channels (the different basic colors that comprise the image).

Background

The background begins with a new and separate layer that can be returned to and corrected in case a different background color is needed to provide greater contrast without changing the shape and color of the figure. The green used is a modification of one of the greens of the basic palette contained in the program. As this image shows, the green does not cover the entire background. This is because the lines of the hair create areas that act like lines or borders between selections. Before painting the upper part of the background, the illustrator has to be sure that the area is closed and that the hair and figure are not selected at the same time as the background.

Finishes

The finished illustration presents considerably more detail than the original photograph. This is achieved by the en-largement possibilities that this program offers. The luminous reflections on the backlit locks of hair were created by working with very light-colored and somewhat transparent fine lines on top of the green of the background.

In respect to both detail and color quality, Toni Vidal's work shows great brilliance and a perfect finish.

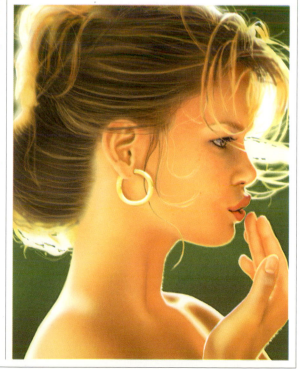

MORE ON THIS SUBJECT
• Computer Illustrations p. 54

COMPUTER TECHNIQUES (II)

The next work illustrated is a fine example of an extremely realistic piece appropriate for a scientific publication (for example, a manual on types of marine crustaceans) or as part of a broader group of graphic elements intended for advertising.

Initial Drawing

The drawing for this subject is copied from a photograph. It is composed of very careful lines that communicate as effectively as possible the peculiarities of the animal's irregular outline. The lines are done in red, the dominant color throughout the shell.

The illustrator chose this color so that the lines of the drawing would blend imperceptibly into the final result. The background is not a separate layer of the drawing but has been left blank so it does not detract from the pain-

Scanners

The great realism goes beyond photographic effect. The interplay of textures multiplies the shines, reflections and satiny, moist qualities–something direct photography cannot do. It could be produced by using the computer to retouch a scanned photographic image. By working freehand, the illustrator choos-es what is important in the illustration without being tied to the nature of the original photograph. From the start the illustrator has sought the grea-test detail, introducing small lines to contrast gradations in the shell's color and lusters playing on it. Some outlines are gone over with a nearly white line to create a luminous effect so precise that it seems unreal.

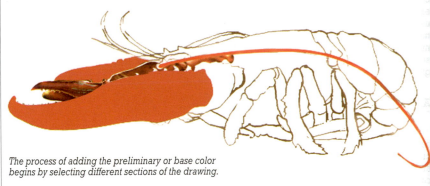

The process of adding the preliminary or base color begins by selecting different sections of the drawing.

Different sprays are added to the existing color base to create the more elaborate textures of the shell.

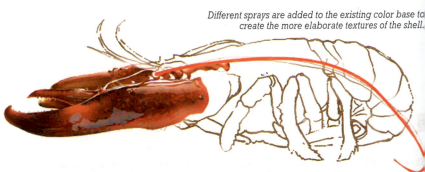

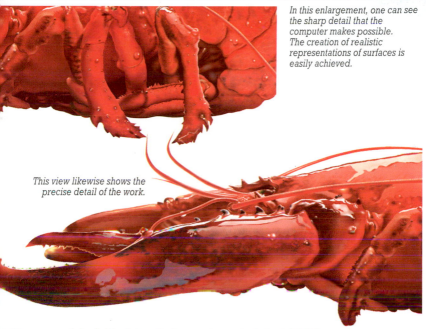

In this enlargement, one can see the sharp detail that the computer makes possible. The creation of realistic representations of surfaces is easily achieved.

This view likewise shows the precise detail of the work.

staking nature of the finished illustration. This image also shows the beginnings of the coloring: the red of the claw is exactly the same as the one used in the drawing. The fragmented nature of the drawing makes it possible to work section by section and pay greater attention to detail.

Areas and Lines

Slowly, the work progresses section by section along the crustacean, bringing each area to the highest degree of completion.

Each area is worked by adding distinct lines either with a "pen" (drawing directly with a uniform line) or by selecting the outline automatically in cases where the line coincides entirely with the outlines of the drawing.

The illustrator saves all these drawings in the computer's memory in order to return to them whenever necessary and highlight or modify them according to the general appearance that the work takes on.

Finishes

The completion of the illustration has involved several returns to previous drawings to adjust the hues and enrich the complex surface. Not only are the color gradations important but the lusters and the shadows reflected by the many articulations are also. The antennas have also been created using strokes where the shadows were subsequently reinforced or softened as the rest of the body was being painted. In short, this is a magnificent illustration carried to the limits of technical perfection.

Shines, transparencies, reflections. . . . All the effects of airbrush are represented to the maximum by the computer in the hands of Toni Vidal.

Note: The titles that appear at the top of the odd-numbered
pages correspond to:

The previous chapter
The current chapter
The following chapter